Overcoming Temptation

Effective Strategies for defeating Temptation

Manickam Chandrakumar

Take note that the name satan and related names are not capitalized. We choose not to acknowledge him, even to the point of violating grammatical rules.

DESTINY IMAGE EUROPE

Via Maiella, 1

66020 San Giovanni Teatino (Ch) - Italy

ISBN:88-89127-03-1

First printing : 2004

This book and all other Destiny Image Europe books are available at Christian bookstores and distributors worldwide.

To order products, or for any other correspondence :

DESTINY IMAGE EUROPE

Via Acquacorrente, 6

65123 Pescara - Italy

Tel. +39 085 4716623 - Fax : +39 085 4716622

E-mail : info@eurodestinyimage.com

Or reach us on the Internet:

www.eurodestinyimage.com

Table Of Contents

1. The Source of Temptation 1
2. The System of Temptation 7
3. The Strategy to Overcome Temptation 13
4. How to Cool Your Sex Urge? 21
5. Joseph's Victory Over Temptation 35
6. Jesus' Victory Over Temptation 47
7. Samson Played With His Anointing 55
8. David Inhaled the Flame of Passion 65
9. Boundaries for Self Control 77
10. How to Overcome Online Temptation 83

Introduction

Temptation is by no means a new or a modern problem. It's as old as Eve and the serpent. "It sometimes seems to us that life is nothing but a series of temptations. As soon as one temptation is overcome, another comes to take its place. It never seems to end," says Edwin D. Roels.

Doesn't the time ever come when our struggle with temptation is forever done away? Unfortunately, that time never comes-at least not during our time on earth.

God has not promised that there would be no temptations in our lives, but He has promised to give us the strength to win a victory over every one of them. There is a way of escape!

Temptation is the root cause of sin. We fall into sin through temptation. Every person in this world, including believers in Christ, suffer temptation. The one who claims otherwise is being untruthful. Jesus Himself was tempted in the wilderness.

The purpose of this book is to uncover the truths about temptation and how to resist it in an easy, simple, and direct approach by examining the Scripture's promises. In its attempt to explain the root cause of the malaise of the people in our own day, this book surveys appropriate examples in the Bible and supplies relevant explanations.

This book is personal in nature. With the necessary grace and an unapologetic honesty, Dr. M. Chandrakumar reveals the truths behind temptation, with the hope that the children of God will live victorious Christian lives, regardless of their individual struggles.

Chapter 1
The Source of Temptation

Temptation comes from satan. God does test us, but satan tempts us. *"Let no man say when he is tempted, I am tempted of God: for God cannot be tempted with evil, neither tempteth he any man: but every man is tempted, when he is drawn away of his own lust, and enticed"* (Jas. 1:13,14).

Satan tempts us to pull us down. God tests us to build us up. Temptation is not sin, for Christ was tempted as we are, yet He remained sinless (see Heb. 4:15). Temptation becomes sin only as we yield to the suggestion of evil. God tests His people by putting them in situations that reveal the quality of their faith and devotion, so that all can see what is in their hearts. (See Genesis 22:1 and Exodus 16:4.) By thus testing them, He purifies them as metal is purified in the refiner's crucible (see 1 Pet.1:6-7).

Satan tests God's people by manipulating their circumstances, within the limits that God allows him, in an attempt to draw them out of God's will. We are responsible for our own temptation. Every one is tempted when he or she is carried away and enticed by his or her own lust (see Jas. 1:14). There are three spheres from where we may expect temptation to come.

1. It may come through the world around us.
2. It may come through the lust within us.
3. It may come into the mind unexpectedly, directly from the devil (see Eph. 6:11-13).

These are the three main lines of attack. Let us consider them one by one.

Temptations That Come Through "The World" (1 John 2:15-17)

Temptation (peirasmos - peirasmoV) means trials. Temptation happens throughout the course of one's life. Temptation affects people both physically and spiritually. A man is tempted to sin, meaning that he sets himself in pride above the limits set for him by God. Temptations that come through the world arise primarily from our environment. We are prone to be affected by the environments in which we live. Fellowship with certain people, geographical location, and personal circumstances are all world-related factors that affect us when we are tempted.

Every time we say no to temptation, we are strengthened, but every time we say yes, we are weakened. Unless there's a real desire to overcome temptation, victory is impossible. Temptations may come from the most unexpected persons and places, and strike at the most unexpected hours. No one should ever say that he would never be tempted in a particular area. You will be tempted strongly to commit that sin against which you have vehemently preached. You will be shaken in that area where you have strengthened others. Seek God's help daily and stay watchful.

Do not love the world or anything in the world. If anyone loves the world, the love of the Father is not in him (1 Jn.2:15).

Anyone who chooses to be a friend of the world becomes an enemy of God (Jas. 4:4b).

We find many examples in the Bible of people who are tempted. For example, King David, the great king of Israel, was tempted to commit (and did commit) adultery with Bathsheba, the wife of one of his soldiers. We read in Second Samuel 11:1, *"Then it happened in the spring, at the time when kings go out to battle, that David sent Joab and his servants with him and all Israel... But David stayed at Jerusalem."*

First, David should not have stayed in Jerusalem. He should have gone to the battlefield. It was the season for kings to go to battle and David was supposed to fight this battle to fulfill God's purpose. David opened himself to this temptation because he failed to be busy in the Lord's work. He was lazily sleeping on his bed in the afternoon. Second, he should not have gone to the roof just to wile away his time. Instead, he could have spent that time praying for those who were battling for him. But David used his time idly to go to the roof, placing himself in the wrong place at the wrong time. David never planned to commit this sin, but he allowed himself to be in the wrong place by his idleness. Neither did Simon Peter think that he would deny Christ. Nonetheless, he allowed himself to stray, unprepared, into a situation that lent itself to that temptation. He was neither going close to Jesus nor was he with the other disciples. He was all alone, wandering about without the fellowship of any other disciple of Christ. The devil is very quick to use such opportunities to tempt us.

The Bible calls the devil the author of temptation, and says that temptation is entirely against God. The tempter is always the enemy of God. Second, by tempting people, the enemy of God shows his power, which is not the will of God. Temptation, used by the enemy, is a power that is stronger than any creature. If the devil is the tempter, then no creature can withstand temptation in his own strength. He must fall. So great is the power of satan (see Eph. 6:12). However, He that is in you is stronger than he that is in the world.

Third, temptation is a seduction, or a leading astray. It is of the devil, for he is a liar (see Jn. 8:44). We fall into the temptations of "the world":

1. When we lower our standards to the level of unbelievers around us.

2. When we begin to be afraid of what other people would think and try to live to please others.
3. When we set our hearts on earthly wealth or fame or honor.

Consciously or unconsciously, humans are tempted in life. Temptation is a reality. It is a universal force, affecting every person. In this modern and technological world, temptation happens without regard to caste, color, position, sex, and age. The world is full of temptation. To be tempted is human. It is natural.

The Temptations That Come Through "The Flesh"

These temptations arise primarily from our passions and desires. They are not separated from the temptation of the world because it is the "flesh" within us, which responds to temptation from outside. However, the source of the temptation is within us, in the form of lust. What do we actually mean by lust? It is "over desire." Desire something is not sin, but "over desire," or lusting after it, is sin. For example, hunger is a desire for food, which, in itself, is not bad. "Over desire" is the lusting to eat more than is necessary, which is the sin of gluttony. Another example is the sex drive in man, which, in itself, is not bad. It is a normal desire to enjoy the bodily pleasures given by God. It is holy in the sight of God. When this desire crosses the boundaries set by God, it becomes lust, the perversion of natural desire. God has set a boundary for every desire of our heart and the temptation to cross this boundary leads us to sin.

Temptation is the awakening of a normal desire by the enemy, with the intention that you satisfy that desire in a way that is unholy. This is why satan suggests to us to think, "Nobody will know," or "It is nobody's business what I do."

Lust of the Flesh

Our natural inclination, which is both sudden and fierce, is to desire. All at once a secret, smoldering fire is kindled. The flesh burns and is in flames. Whether it is sexual desire, ambition, vanity, the desire for revenge, the greed for money, the love of fame and power, or that strange desire for the beautiful things of the world, the lust thus aroused envelops the mind and will of man in deepest darkness. Our discernment and decision-making abilities are weakened at this point. All kinds of questions come into our minds: "Is what the flesh desires really sin in this case? Is it really not permitted to me to appease my desire?" The tempter puts us in a privileged position as he once tried to urge the hungry Son of God to change stones into bread (see Lk. 4:1-4). We boast of our privileges that can sometimes be against God.

There is only one reality stronger than our desire and of satan's influence and that is the image and the presence of the Crucified. Against this power, the power of desire dissolves into nothingness, for here it is conquered. Here, the flesh has received its right and reward, namely, death. We read in James 1:15, "When lust has conceived it gives birth to sin; and when sin is accomplished, it brings forth death." The lust of the flesh is nothing else than the anguish of the flesh in the face of death. Only the death of Christ rescues us from the temptation of the flesh.

Attitude of the heart

We need to consider one more important aspect of lust. It is primarily the attitude of the heart. God told lucifer in Isaiah 14:13-14, "But you said in your heart, 'I will ascend to heaven; I will raise my throne above the stars of God... I will make myself like the most high." Even before lucifer could talk or put into action what he thought, God caught him in his attitudes. Jesus says, in Matthew 5:28, "anyone who looks at a woman lustfully has already committed adultery with her in his heart." So, temptation and sin are matters of the heart.

The Temptations That Come Directly Into "The Mind"

Sometimes evil thoughts come into our minds that have nothing to do with our surroundings or feelings. We need to realize that satan can tempt us independently of the world around us, or of the lusts within us. We know from Ephesians 6:16 that he can hurl one of his fiery darts into the mind at any time. We also read in Psalms 64:4b, "*they shoot at him suddenly, without fear." And in Ecclesiastes* 9:12,

"Moreover, man does not know his time: like fish caught in a treacherous net and birds trapped in a snare, so the sons of men are ensnared at an evil time when it suddenly falls on them."

The Most Important Requirements

1. We need to pray that in the hour of temptation, which is bound to come, strength may be given to us to overcome temptation.

2. We must be able to recognize the temptations that come through the world around us and try to avoid putting ourselves in tempting situations. Sometimes, in certain situations and circumstances, we may not be able to avoid certain temptations, but if we recognize them, with the help of the Lord, we can overcome them.

3. We must be able to recognize the temptations of the flesh and we must starve the desires of the body. They grow stronger each time they are indulged in and weaker each time they are denied. The severity of our temptations will increase as the capacity of our endurance increases. No temptation can overtake us. Our God is faithful to us. Therefore, He will not let us be tempted beyond our strength, but with temptation He will also provide the way of escape that we may be able to endure it (see 1 Cor.10:13). (Deeply dedicated people of God can be more severely tested than new believers in Christ. Mother Theresa told one lady that she was suffering because God loved her. The lady replied, "Please ask God not to love me so much.")

4. We must be able to recognize the temptations of the devil and resist him so that he will flee from us (Jas. 4:7b).

Chapter 2
The System Of Temptation

Through Deception

The system that satan often uses to tempt us is through deception. Sometimes satan uses the Scriptures to deceive us. He used them to tempt Jesus in the wilderness. To fight against this temptation, Jesus did not use his own words or thoughts. He too used appropriate scriptures to counter satan's attack. Unless we have a thorough grasp of at least some of the important commands and promises of the Scriptures, satan can easily deceive us.

Even in tempting Eve, satan started with the scriptures. He asked her in Genesis 3:1, *"Indeed, has God said, 'You shall not eat from any tree of the garden'?"* He slightly twisted the command of God. This, to some extent, caused Eve to stumble. When she quoted God's command, she added that she and Adam may not even "touch it," which God had not originally told them (see Gen. 3:3). Following this, satan completely reverses the command, saying, "You surely shall not die!" He then entices her by saying that in the day they eat from it their eyes will be opened and they will be like God, knowing good and evil (see Gen. 3:4-5). This is exactly what Satan is doing even today. He is giving, mainly to young people, false hopes and assurances. He induces a spirit of ease in them, encouraging them to live as they please, convincing them that nothing will affect them. Satan is always behind us trying to entice us and deceive us. He has worked out many strategies to keep people away from God. "God never tempts any man. That is Satan's business" (Billy Graham).

A story is told of satan once holding a committee meeting of his missionaries. President lucifer complained about not winning many souls into his kingdom. The general secretary came out with the following proposal. He said, "I will go to the earth and tell the people that the Bible is not true and there was no man called Jesus." Lucifer bluntly replied that he would not be successful. Then the coordinator of missions stood up and said, "I will go and confuse the people and make them very busy doing various other things and tell them not be concerned about religion." Lucifer was not happy with this plan either. Then an ordinary, humble committee member stood up and said, "I will go and tell the people that the Bible is true and that there was a man called Jesus, but you need not worry or hurry to do something about it in your life now. You can relax and take it easy. Since you are young, you need to enjoy the world. There are many more things, which you have not tasted. So, first enjoy the thrills of this world and then later on you can think of religion. God is not going to run away anywhere. He will wait for you." Lucifer was very pleased with this proposal, approved it, and even promoted this ordinary committee member to be his personal secretary. From this illustration, we understand that deception in the hands of satan is a powerful weapon that he uses to cause many people to stumble.

Through Thrilling Experiences

Today, young people are looking for thrilling experiences. Satan seems to have an endless supply of these. Perhaps, even in his first attempt to entice mankind to fall into temptation, he may have used a thrilling experience. We do not read in the creation story that snakes were talking creatures, but one day probably, when Eve was playing with the snakes, suddenly one of them might have turned around and said "Hey Eve how are you? Did God tell you this?" So, Eve might have been caught up in this thrilling experience of talking with a snake. While she was distracted with the talking serpent, his twisting of the Lord's command completely confused her, causing her to believe satan's word instead. Today, many people are easily carried away by their or others' experiences, rather than deeply considering them and being influenced by the Word of God. So, satan is undoubtedly a deceiver and the father of lies. Because of this, we should be all the more careful of becoming unnecessarily focused the thrilling moments in life. Doctor C. I. Scofield, writing of the evangelist Mr. Moody, calls attention to his strength and faithfulness under the trial of temptation:

"Three supreme testings await strong men in this life… the testing of poverty and obscurity, of prosperity and applause, and of suffering. Many, who enter life conscious, even though dimly, of great latent capacities turn sour and bitter under neglect, narrow circumstances, and lack of appreciation. Others who pass that first trial successfully are corrupted or enfeebled by success and adulation. Many who stand erect alike in obscurity and success fail utterly under the testing of suffering. By God's grace, Mr. Moody passed unscathed through them all. Perhaps it has happened to few men, suddenly lifted into the fellowship of the noble and famous of the earth, to be so little moved from the serenity of their minds, the even tenor of their ways".

Through Experimentation

Young people today are on the brink of a new age of commercialization of life itself. With the emerging electronic media, in entertainment and business, the uni-lateral move of globalization, and the accessibility of communication facilities all over the globe, the youth of today are experiencing a new way of life.

Media plays a great role in setting standards of living, fads, and fashions that are projected as the popular thing to do. Advertisement and marketing agencies have increasingly concentrated on college-going youth as the crowd that falls for their allurements. Consumer products have lately been marketed to cater to the needs of young people, the elite, and the rich. The youth of today are tempted to imitate and experiment with each one of them as they are flaunted in print and on electronic media. As they subtly experiment with this new way of life, very few are aware of the possibility of becoming addicted. Those who experiment with such trends as the "in-thing" eventually develop, out of addiction, the need for continued financial backing, to support this way of life. If the finances are not immediately forthcoming, it then becomes tempting for the youth to resort to unseemly, immoral means to gaining the necessary finances, as is the case with any addict. Thus, experimenting with worldly lifestyle leads to unsavory habits and untrustworthy friends.

Experimentation is not wrong in itself. We do things by trial and error. We learn from mistakes. However, if life remains as mere experimentation, it needs to be governed and guided. Thus the youth of today, as well as all others, need an effective introduction to moral and spiritual living, which will enable them to make the right choices and do the right things, according to Scripture. Young people, for example, need particular direction when making decisions regarding careers, friends, and spouses. Such decisions are based primarily out of one's upbringing. This means that parents should be mostly responsible for helping their children work through their decisions.

The spiritual or the moral upbringing of a child begins at home with the parents. The moral and spiritual training they had at home remains their strength and upholds their moral choices in life. With such a foundation in place, young people then need to openly encounter situations that test their integrity and moral fiber. They need to wrestle during time of temptation throughout life so that they learn to choose the abundant life found in Christ. Spiritual integrity and maturity comes from studying the word of God. If one is built on that foundation in Christ, he or she is able to withstand any sufferings, including temptation, which is the lure of evil.

Through Exposure

You have been exposed to a different kind of life before committing your lives to Christ. But now, with Christ in your lives, you need to be exposed to a new phase of life in spite of temptation and the evil desires around us. You cannot be your own savior, either in whole or in part. Hudson Taylor says:

"I cannot tell you how I am buffeted sometimes by temptation. I never knew how bad a heart I have. Yet I do know that I love God and love His work, and desire to serve Him only and in all things. And I value above all else that precious Savior in whom alone I can be accepted. Often I am tempted to think that one so full of sin cannot be a child of God at all. But I try to throw it back, and rejoice all the more in the precariousness of Jesus and in the riches of the grace that has made us 'accepted in the beloved.' Beloved He is of God; beloved He ought to be of us. But oh, how short I fall here again! May God help me to love Him more and serve Him better. Do pray for me. Pray that the Lord will keep me from sin, will sanctify me wholly, will use me more largely in His service".

Parents need to expose their children to different ways of living as they might present various career paths for them. Doing this enables them to choose the right things for themselves and for their future. In order to make the correct decisions about living for Christ, both parents and children need to have a healthy exposure to different aspects of religious, moral, and social life.

Our families need to be built on the foundation of Christ. Love, peace, and truth should prevail in the family. If children are brought up in that atmosphere of love, openness, and integrity of character, they will be more confident to face difficult situations in their adult lives. These virtues need to be integrated into life with the spiritual fervor that is desired by God in Christ.

[illegible]

Through it most [illegible]

[illegible] have been [illegible] and your [illegible] to a new phase of life [illegible] your [illegible]. You [illegible] particularly [illegible].

[illegible] cover [illegible] to know [illegible] and [illegible] something [illegible] can be accepted [illegible] the [illegible] the [illegible] of the grace [illegible] to the [illegible] and [illegible] largely [illegible].

Parents [illegible] different ways [illegible] as they [illegible] the [illegible] of [illegible] and [illegible] in order to [illegible] to [illegible] of religious, moral and social life.

[illegible] of Christ's love, peace and [illegible] of [illegible] of character [illegible] will [illegible] which [illegible] God in Christ.

Chapter 3
The Strategy To Overcome Temptation

The Strategies

1. Recognize Your Inclination Towards Sin

The first and most important strategy used to overcome sin and temptation is to admit, like Paul in Romans 7:18, "For I know that nothing good dwells in me, that is, in my flesh. . . ." We need to realize and acknowledge that we are weak people.

"Therefore let him who thinks he stands take heed lest he fall." (1 Cor. 10:12).

First, Paul opposes all false security, and second, he opposes all false despondency in the face of temptation. Though we have become partakers of the divine nature, we have not completely lost our old nature. Also, we are always surrounded by the presence of sin. So the old nature cannot be completely eradicated around us, but it can and must be eradicated within us.

No one can be sure, even for a moment, that he can remain free from temptation. There is no temptation that could not attack us suddenly, without warning. No one should think that satan is far from him. *"Be of sober spirit, be on the alert. Your adversary, the devil, prowls around like a roaring lion, seeking someone to devour."* (1 Pet. 5:8). *"Keep watching and praying that you may not enter into temptation..."* (Matt. 26:41).

Every temptation can be resisted. You must watch and pray, avoiding situations in which you know you are likely to be tempted. Be on guard against the crafty enemy, and ask the Lord to hold you fast in His Word and in His Grace.

2. Reckon Yourself "Dead to Sin"

As we read in Romans 6:1-2, you must consider yourself dead to sin and alive to God. In practical terms, it means to learn to be so absorbed in the companionship of Christ that the enticements of sin will pass you by. There are some flowers that, even when in bloom, close up during the night. When the sun shines on them, they open again to its life-giving rays. They are dead to the dark and alive to the light, closed to one and open to the other.

3. Starve your 'Old Nature'

A criminal nailed to a cross was reckoned as dead even while he still lived. As long as he remained on the cross he was powerless to do evil. That is how your old nature should be treated. Paul says in Galatians 5:24, *"Now those who belong to Christ Jesus have crucified the flesh with its passions and desires."* He further says, *"I have been crucified with Christ; it is no longer I who live, but Christ lives in me..."* (Gal. 2:20). So, if you have crucified your old nature, then you will plan your activities in a way that will make no provision for stimulating the old desires. We read in Romans 13:14, *"...make no provision for the flesh in regard to its lusts."*

The root cause of a particular sin into which you have fallen must be discovered and eliminated from your life. We read in Acts 19:19 that many magicians received Christ and soon after that they burned their magic books which cost them fifty thousand pieces of silver (several thousand dollars). Likewise you must ruthlessly starve the old nature of those things on which it feeds. Only then it is possible to rob it of its power and prepare the way for victory over temptation.

4. Feed your "New Nature"

You must feed your new nature in Christ with the Word of God, which includes reading spiritual books other than the Scriptures. Spending much time in prayer and maintaining constant fellowship with other believers is also necessary.

The Process of Sin and Temptation

Let us carefully consider the process of sin and temptation and how to tactfully escape from it. In considering the process of sin, Theodore H. Epp says, "Lust is the Bud, Sin is the Blossom, and Death is the Fruit." That is why it is important to nip temptation in the bud. It must be stopped before it can blossom into sin and death. The key to responding to temptation is to be prepared in advance before it comes. Jesus knew that He was about to be tempted and made Himself ready.

When a sinful desire enters the mind, it will grow until the deed is executed, if it is not checked at once. As a rule, the mind eventually acts out what it dwells on. David is an example of this truth. First he saw a beautiful woman bathing, and then he delighted in what he saw. We can call this the second look. This second look is always very dangerous. Because he allowed his mind to dwell on what he saw, the delight turned into desire that we call lust. This desire brought about a decision to fulfill that lust and thus, he deliberately committed sin with Bathsheba, resulting in the death of her husband and of her first son, born through David. Because he did not nip temptation in the bud, he went on to put his thoughts into action and fell into sin.

Let us consider some more examples from the Bible that show how lust brought about sin, which resulted in death. The process that led Eve to the eating of the fruit is recorded in Genesis 3:6. First, there was the lust, or desire for the forbidden fruit. Then thoughts turned into action to produce sin, and sin produced death. Spiritual death was immediate, and resulted in eventual physical death. Notice the progress: she saw that the fruit was pleasant. As we discussed earlier, she had a second look by allowing her mind to dwell on what she saw. Then she desired; she took and she ate.

Let us compare Eve's yielding to temptation in Genesis 3:6 with 1 John 2:16. First, Eve saw that the tree was good for food. This is what John calls as the "lust of the flesh." It is a craving for gratifying the sensual needs of the flesh. Food and sex are the main constituents of this craving. Second, she saw that it was a delight to the eyes. John calls this the "lust of the eyes." It is a greedy longing of the mind. Third, she saw that the tree was desirable to make one wise. John calls this as the boastful "pride of life." He says that this is not from the Father, but is from the world.

Thus the process satan uses to tempt a believer is to get him absorbed into the world's system. Slowly, the material blessings that the world offers would become the central desire of the believer. The honor and recognition of this world would become his important goal. In order to live a comfortable and secure life, he would even compromise with the worldly systems.

The process that led Achan to sin is recorded in Joshua 7:21. Achan said,

When I saw in the plunder a beautiful robe from Babylonia, two hundred shekels of silver, and a wedge of gold weighing fifty shekels, then I coveted them, and took them. They are hidden in the ground inside my tent, with the silver underneath.

Notice the progress. He saw, coveted, took, and hid.

God has done His part by supplying you with a new potential to resist temptation (the new inner self) and the power source to activate that nature (the Holy Spirit). Your responsibility is to continuously act in faith on His promises and to expect victory. To withstand satan's demonic forces, God has given you His Word and the fellowship of His children. Therefore, adopt a new outlook on life. Put aside the thought that spiritual defeat is inevitable. Recognize instead that victory is certain. You can overcome temptation!

The Ways Of Escape

1. Flee From Evil

The Bible teaches us that at times of temptation in the flesh we must flee: "fornication" (1 Cor. 6:18), "idolatry" (1 Cor. 10:14), "youthful lusts" (2 Tim. 2:22), "the lust of the world" (2 Pet. 1:4), and other forms of sexual immorality.

All other sins a man commits are outside his body, but he who sins sexually sins against his own body. Do you not know that your body is a temple of the Holy Spirit, who is in you, whom you have received from God? You are not your own; you were bought at a price. Therefore honor God with your body (1 Cor. 6:18-20).

The Greek word for "sexual immorality" is porneia. This is the word from which the English word "pornography" is derived. Pornography is one of the major sources of sexual information that most young people have about sexuality, and has therefore become the central mechanism by which their sexuality has been constructed. It is a trap you should avoid as much as possible. Dwelling upon pornographic thoughts often results in action.

A person can be sexually aroused through sight. This means that one should always be alert by guarding his eyes. No one can help what is seen accidentally, but everyone can control the mind from dwelling on a temptation and from taking a second or extended look. Eve, Achan, Samson, and David fell into sin through what they saw. Every person is responsible to God to use his or her body as God intends.

There is no resistance to satan other than flight. Every struggle against lust in one's own strength is doomed to failure. The word "flee" can indeed only mean that you must flee to that place where you find protection and help, flee to the crucified Jesus who is alive today. His image and His presence alone can help. We have the great privilege of sharing the victory of Jesus against Satan upon the cross. We can rely on the faithfulness of God and He will keep us from the hour of temptation (see 1 Cor. 1:9; 10:13; Rev. 3:10).

2. Use The Word Of God

Jesus himself was tempted in everything, exactly as we are, and yet he was without sin (see Heb. 4:15). Satan tempted Jesus in the same way he tempted Eve (see Lk. 4:1-13). He tempts us at the right time. When Jesus was hungry, satan tried to induce the lust of the flesh in Jesus by asking him to turn the stones into bread. By promising the kingdom of the earth, he tried to induce in Jesus the lust of the eyes. By challenging him at the pinnacle of the temple, he tried to induce in Jesus the pride of life. Although satan used the Word of God to tempt Jesus, Jesus also used the Word of God to get victory over this temptation. Through this example, we know that the Word of God is an important tool in overcoming temptation.

3. Hate Sin

You cannot have victory over sin and temptation unless you hate sin. As long as you delight in a particular sin, you can never get victory over it. Following is an illustration of this principle.

The monkey catchers, first of all, dig a very narrow hole in the ground, just big enough for the monkey's hand to fit inside. They then widen the bottom of the hole so that the monkey can open and stretch out the palm. Into these holes they place groundnuts, which monkeys often eat. Then they hide behind the trees some distance away with sticks and nets in their hands. The monkeys can easily smell the groundnuts. They place their hands into these holes and grab as many groundnuts as they can. The problem they face is that they cannot take their hands out while grabbing the groundnuts. They shout and struggle but still cannot take their hands out. At this point, the monkey catchers simply come and put the nets over them. Even then, the monkeys will not let the groundnuts go and the monkey catchers start beating them with their sticks. Because of their unwillingness to let go of the groundnuts, the monkeys are captured.

Satan also is ready to capture you with his net. You too might have some "groundnuts" in your life that you want to hold on to, perhaps lusting after certain things that are dear to you, or indulging in sensual habits. Are you willing to let go of these "groundnuts"? Unless you hate them, you will not let them go. There is no use in just praying to God for victory over sin and temptation without first hating sin. With real hatred towards sin in your heart, you must go into the presence of God and plead with him for the victory, and then only will He grant you victory.

4. Be Aware of satan's Schemes

It is important for us to know the tactics that the enemy uses against us so that we are not outwitted by him (see 2 Cor. 2:11).

a. He is a liar (see Jn. 8:44).

b. He is a slanderer and accuser (see Rev. 12:10).

c. He is a deceiver (see Rev. 12:9).

d. He is a tempter (see Matt. 4:1-11).

e. He is an oppressor (see Acts 10:38).

f. He is a hinderer (see 1 Thess. 2:18).

g. He is a roaring lion (see 1 Pet. 5:8).

h. He can transform himself into an angel of light (see 2 Cor. 11:14).

God fights for us in times of temptation. Spurgeon says,

"If that roaring lion that goes about continually seeking whom he may devour finds us alone among the vineyards of the Philistines, where is our hope? Not in our heels, for he is swifter than we; not in our weapons, for we are naturally unarmed; not in our hands, which are weak and languishing; but in the Spirit of God, by whom we can do all things. Who can ever resist us if God fights in us? There is a stronger lion in us than that against us."

To be tempted is human; to overcome temptation is divine. One must make conscious efforts to control and overcome temptation. To do so, we must have faith, trust, confidence, and a willingness to obey the God. The first man was tempted and disobeyed God by breaking the commandment of God. The second Man was also tempted, but overcame temptation by obeying God even unto the point of His death on the cross. God knows that you need a power greater than yourself to withstand satan, so He has provided Himself, living in you.

"Greater is He who is in you than he who is in the world" (1 Jn. 4:4).

The apostle Paul revealed how God equips believers to face satan and his demons. He first speaks about the Christian's defensive weapons

"The...strong belt of truth and the breastplate of God's approval. Wear shoes that speed you on as you preach the Good News of peace with God. In every battle you will need faith as your shield to stop the fiery arrows aimed at you by satan. You will also need the helmet of salvation....

" He then adds the one offensive weapon-"and the sword of the Spirit-which is the Word of God" (see Eph. 6:14-17).

Chapter 4
How To Cool Your Sex Urge?

In these last days we live in a sexually, emotionally, and racially super-charged climate. Many times we are tempted to go too far, too soon, mentally and physically. When the flame of passion starts burning in us, how do we quench it?

Fantasy Gives Way To Action

You go to bed at night and your imagination begins to run wild with unholy thoughts. You say, "Well, it's not doing me any harm. It's not affecting any one else." And you succumb to temptation and end up in masturbation. You do not put up any fight at all. You fall because you fail to say, "This is no way for a child of God to act. My body is the temple of the Holy Spirit. My standards are higher than this, so I will not do it."

Society teaches us that anything done privately between two consenting adults is acceptable. But if sex is free, then why is it costing the society so much? What two consenting adults do in private involves us all. Tragically, today's youth are being led to believe that there's no cost involved. The modern day message that pounds into their lives is:

"It's easy, it's free, it's fun. If you feel like it, great! Go ahead and do it." Even in schools, the concept of "safe sex with condoms" is very much taught, and the careful usage of different types of condoms is widely demonstrated.

In movies you see the hero taking his girlfriend to bed, and you may regard it as a natural part of life. It excites you and you too want to experience it. No one tells you that pre-marital sex affects you emotionally, psychologically, economically, medically, and spiritually. It ruins you physically and mentally. Pre-marital sex is sin, and a person just can't be a friend with God if he is going to continue to sin deliberately and willfully. God has said, *"You shall not commit adultery."* This is one of the Ten Commandments. But the world has rewritten and presented them to us as the Ten Amendments. God says lawlessness is sin, witchcraft is an abomination, and sex outside of marriage is prohibited. Yet three top-selling paperbacks of the 1970s were, *The Godfather,* which deals with crime; *The Exorcist,* concerning demonism; and *Love Story,* which glorifies fornication.

Personal pleasure makes a good slave but a poor master. When our primary focus is on self-gratification, the results are not only destructive to us, but also to everyone around us (see Titus 3:3; Jas. 4:1-4). Scripture makes it clear that living for our own pleasures is both unacceptable and unhealthy. We read in Old Testament history that, when young Shechem saw the beautiful girl Dinah, he allowed his lust to rule his behavior and he raped her. Like an animal, he let his hormones run his life to the point that sexual gratification became more important than Dinah's dignity as a person. (see Gen. 34:2). By contrast, Scripture challenges God's people to exercise control over their sexuality (see 1 Thess. 4:3-4). Our biological needs, such as food, sex, and sleep, are important. When we allow these to run our lives, they tend to become vicious addictions that destroy us. And each time we're confronted with a sinful compulsive desire, the choice we make demonstrates our level of spiritual strength.

Sexual passion can be powerful and beautiful, but to keep it from drowning away, it needs to be fenced in by commitment, discipline, and self-control. Our sexuality is not our own. It is a gift from God to be treasured and used for His glory (see 1 Cor. 6:18-20).

God's View Of Sex

First of all, we must have an understanding of what the Scriptures say about sex. It is holy in the sight of God. It is created and ordained by God (see Gen. 2:24). The Bible says,

"May your fountain be blessed, and may you rejoice in the wife of your youth. A loving doe, a graceful deer-may her breasts satisfy you always, may you ever be captivated by her love." (Prov. 5:18-19).

Paul said to abstain from sexual immorality (see Acts 15:20).

We are born in sin and thus, we have a sinful nature. Sexual immorality is a part of this sinful nature (see Gal. 5:19). Through the help of the Holy Spirit we must get victory over this sinful nature. Paul says that there should not be even a hint of sexual immorality or any kind of impurity among God's holy people (see Eph. 5:3). God created people to experience sex within the covenant of marriage, which involves a commitment to the whole person. It is very clear that sex is holy, honorable, acceptable, and enjoyable only within the framework of marriage, which is a sacrament of love and grace. This love is sealed by sexuality, and sexuality, in turn, needs this love to function with integrity. It is definitely not God's intention for any one to have any kind of sexual excitement outside of the marriage relationship.

Since God desires that a husband and wife should have an intimate relationship with each other, to live in a relationship filled with unconfessed sin, secret struggles, and hidden failures cannot nurture intimacy. Confession may cause pain and disappointment, but without full disclosure, the marriage cannot be authentic and will never become the type of relationship that God has designed for us. In addition, your spouse can be one of your most valuable means of accountability, and may provide you with significant strength and motivation.

The physical delights of married love have been greatly dramatized by the Song of Solomon. In this passionate love song between a king and his bride, both revel in praising and caressing the other's body, and affirming the sanctity of marriage by giving us a healthy picture of God's love for His people. The writer of the book of Hebrews plants a protective hedge around a husband and a wife's sexual intimacy, warning,

"let the marriage bed be undefiled; for fornicators and adulterers God will judge" (Heb. 13:4).

Fornication and adultery are both acts outside the boundary of marriage. They represent erotic lust--improper, illicit, or unnatural expressions of sexual involvement. Those who are involved in such acts cannot legitimately and whole-heartedly enjoy the pure gift of sex with one's marital partner. These powerful sensations can grab hold of your mind, whether married or not, and turn the blessing of sexual pleasure into a degrading addiction to uncontrollable lusts.

Many young people have found themselves plagued by guilt after they have indulged in intimacies such as petting, kissing, cuddling, embracing, and even holding hands. This being so, obviously the people who are involved in heavy petting, prolonged kissing, mutual masturbation, oral sex, and genital intercourse would all the more feel guilty, insecure, and even develop a hatred towards each other as in the case of Amnon in the Old Testament. He fell in love with his half sister Tamar and, after forcefully having a sexual relationship with her, he hated her more than he had loved her (see 2 Sam. 13:1-19). This is nothing but a deliberate sin against God. No wonder we are punished by venereal diseases, one of which is AIDS, for which there is still no remedy. Many young people who have fallen into such sins neither planned it before, nor even dreamt of falling into such a thing. They were trying to justify themselves saying, "petting is not sin," not realizing that any sexually exciting relationship can lead to the bed room or to a literal intercourse with each other. This is the power of sexual temptation.

The Bible continually warns that sexually immoral people cannot inherit the kingdom of God. Without holiness no one will see the Lord (see Heb. 12:14; Rev. 22:15). Though not all, many believers too show weakness in the area of sex. They get easily drawn to the opposite sex. They find themselves emotionally disturbed and perturbed. They are aware of God's word and his warnings about sexual immorality, but they feel emotionally helpless. The word of God says to abstain from sexual immorality (see Acts 15:29). Paul cautions us not even to associate ourselves with anyone who calls himself a brother, but is sexually immoral (see 1 Cor. 5:9-11).

We are to take care of what belongs to Christ. We must not pollute, defile, degrade, or dishonor His temple. Sexual intimacy unites the total personalities-the mind, will, and emotions-of two individuals. Sexual sin corrupts an individual, violates God's purpose, and defaces God's temple. Sexual immorality affects an individual's total personality.

Practical Steps In Overcoming Temptation

1. Remember that your body does not belong to you. You have been bought with a price-the precious blood of Jesus Christ (see 1 Pet. 1:18-19). Therefore, glorify and honor God with your body (see 1 Cor. 6:18-20).
2. Keep a safe distance away from the opposite sex. Memorize the relevant scripture verses, which would build a barricade against sexual temptations.
3. Avoid going out or staying alone with a person of the opposite sex. Even while counseling, insist that at least two members of the opposite sex should be present.
4. Do not read any book or see any movie that excites sexual thoughts in you. Fill your mind with things that are holy (see Phil. 4:8).
5. Do not keep your mind idle or lie down on your bed with bad thoughts. Pray before you go to bed and keep writing some letters or read some good Christian books until you get to sleep.

6. Ask God to give you the strength and mentality with which you can appreciate and praise God for the loveliness and beauty when you look at a pretty girl or an attractive man. When you praise God for a person, then you cannot lust over that person.

7. Be careful, alert, and conscious at all times (see Eccl. 9:12). Guard your heart and resist temptation. Whenever you find yourself drawn towards any particular person of the opposite sex, do not become overly familiar with that person (see Prov. 4:23). Keep your emotions in check.

8. Remind yourself that any fall in this area would ruin your testimony and your ministry. It will bring shame and disgrace to you, to the person involved, to your families, to the fellowship or the church to which you belong, and to the Lord. The very fact that you would not be able to meet the pain and sorrow in someone's eyes should stop you from attempting to yield to temptation.

9. C. S. Lewis said, "Sexual appetite like any other appetite, grows by indulgence." Hence, do not indulge in lustful looks and thoughts or sexual fantasies. Jesus said that any one who looks at a woman lustfully has already committed adultery with her in his heart (see Matt. 5:28). So, you can be an adulterer in your heart, and you would receive the same punishment from the Lord as the man who indulges in physical adultery.

10. Avoid the second look. Do not linger on or take delight when you look at anything that tempts you mentally or physically. Work hard and keep working until you get rid of this weakness in your character.

11. Keep away from obvious areas of temptation. Keep saying, *"I will set before my eyes no vile thing"* (see Ps. 101:3; 1 Tim. 6:9-11).

12. Keep your focus on the right values in life. *"Since, then, you have been raised with Christ, set your hearts on things above, where Christ is seated at the right hand of God. Set your minds on things above, not on earthly things"* (Col. 3:1-2).

13. Thank God for his promise to deliver you during the time of temptation. Commit yourself to respond to His help, which is always available, so that you can live in victory.

You may think that resisting temptation is some mystical, unreachable, unattainable talent, reserved either for the very old or the very pious. There is nothing magical about it. You have to simply put Jesus Christ at the helm of your life and say "No!" John Wesley once said, "Give me men who love nothing but God and hate nothing but sin." That's it precisely. The Lord will give you the power to say "no" when the tempter comes (see Jas. 4:7)

Counteract temptation. Do not tolerate it. God does not give us only a negative command. No, he says, "Yield yourself to God." In other words, do not try to peacefully coexist with temptation. Come out and go against it. You may play around with things that make you weak. For example: If you are weakened by certain kinds of music, you are playing into the hands of satan himself by listening to it. If you are weakened by certain motion pictures that bring before your eyes things that build lustful desires, which you find difficult to overcome, then you are not counteracting sin and temptation. You are tolerating, fertilizing, and prompting it.

Make a Covenant with your Eyes

You may have to make a commitment with your eyes. Job says, *"I have made a covenant with my eyes; how then could I gaze at a virgin"* (Job 31:1)?

The "eye gate" is a marvel, but it also opens to our experience the floodgates of sensuality. We read in the Bible,

"Let your eyes look directly ahead and let your gaze be fixed straight in front of you" (Prov. 4:25).

We must pay close attention to what we look at. Our eyes seem to be the closest connection to our minds. Through our eyes we bring in information and visual images. Through our eyes we feed our imaginations. Through our eyes we focus on things that are alluring and attractive.

The battle in this world is a battle within the mind, which is the major target of the enemy's appeal. Charles R. Swindoll says,

"When the world pulls back its bowstring, our minds are the bull's-eyes. The arrows we allow to become impaled in our minds will ultimately poison our thoughts. To counter this seduction of the cosmos, we should focus our mind on Christ."

Fix your eyes upon Jesus who is the author and perfector of your faith (see Heb. 12:2).

Present Pleasures or Painful Consequences?

Caution yourself that the final pain will soon erase the temporary pleasure. Moses followed this principle. He chose to walk with God rather than to become absorbed in the attractions and the pleasures of Egypt's lifestyle.

"By faith Moses, when he had grown up, refused to be called the son of Pharaoh's daughter, choosing rather to endure ill-treatment with the people of God, than to enjoy the passing pleasures of sin" (Heb. 11:24-25).

Sin is so pleasurable that people are willing to risk their reputations to taste its flavor. When you turn off the internal warnings, you automatically turn on the desire.

Let the Word of God control your thought life. When the devil launched his full-scale attack against Jesus, He withstood temptation by using the Scriptures. We read in the Bible, *"How can a young man keep his way pure? By keeping it according to Your word... Your word I have treasured in my heart, that I may not sin against You"* (Ps. 119:9,11). When the Word of God is stored up in our minds, it stands ready to strike. No weapon of deception can stand against the truth.

In the wilderness, Jesus knew that life comes from God. He realized that, in His human form, He must keep His eyes on the Father. If you turn your eyes upon Jesus, you will find far more than you were ever looking for. Some people have a wishful thinking that if God would save them and then, within a matter of seconds, take them to heaven, it would be a great relief and they would never have any temptations and would never mess up their lives. They just want to be whisked off to glory - saved, sanctified, galvanized, and glorified! Some have suggested sanctification by isolation. After all, how can you walk through a coal mine without getting dirty?

Jesus prayed for his disciples and for us:

"I have given them Thy word; and the world has hated them, because they are not of the world, even as I am not of the world. I do not ask Thee to take them out of the world, but to keep them from the evil one" (Jn. 17:14-15).

He has left us in the world on purpose and for His purpose. In this dark world where the majority are going the wrong way, we are left as illuminating lights and as living examples of the right way. We are spiritual salmon swimming upstream.

This world is inspired by "the spirit of the age." Trench defines it as follows:

"All that floating mass of thoughts, opinions, maxims, speculations, hopes, impulses, aims, aspirations, at any time current in the world, which it may be impossible to seize and accurately define, but which constitutes a most real and effective power, being the moral, or immoral atmosphere which at every moment of our lives we inhale, again inevitably to exhale."

You must give greater thought to the consequences of sin rather than to its pleasures. If you're thinking about having an affair or if you are being caught in that lustful trap, it would be better for you to walk through the consequences in your mind. Think through the effects of that act in your life and in the lives of others whom your life touches.

Randy Alcorn says that, whenever he is feeling particularly vulnerable to sexual temptation, he finds it helpful to review the effect such actions could have. Some of the things he mentions are:

a. Grieving the Lord who redeemed you...

b. One day having to look at Jesus... in the face and give an account of your actions...

c. Inflicting untold hurt on... your best friend and loyal wife... losing [her] respect and trust.

d. Hurting your beloved daughters...

e. Destroying your example and credibility with your children, and nullifying both present and future efforts to teach them to obey God...

f. Causing shame to your family...

g. Creating a form of guilt that would be hard to shake. Even though God would forgive you, would you forgive yourself?

h. Forming memories and flashbacks that could plague future intimacy with your wife.

i. Wasting years of ministry training and experience…

j. Undermining the faithful example and hard work of other Christians in your community.

k. Bringing great pleasure to satan, the enemy of God and all that is good....

l. Possibly bearing the physical consequences of such diseases as gonorrhea, syphilis, chlamydia, herpes, and AIDS; perhaps infecting your wife or even causing her death.

m. Possibly causing pregnancy, with the personal and financial implications, including a lifelong reminder of your sin...

n. Causing shame and hurt to your friends, especially those you have led to Christ.

And that's just a small list of the consequences! It doesn't even begin to focus on the consequences for the other person in the affair and the number of people affected by his or her sin.

Freedom From Sexual Bondage

It is the truth that sets you free. It's not what you do that sets you free from sexual bondage, but rather, what you believe. According to Romans 6:12-13, you must not let sin reign in your mortal body so that you obey its evil desires. Do not blame the devil. God never commands us to do something we cannot do. The devil can't make you do anything. He will tempt you and try to deceive you, but if sin reigns in your body it is because of you. You are responsible for your actions and downfall.

Having yielded to your temptation and allowed it to happen, how then do you prevent sin from reigning in your body? Paul says, *"Do not offer the parts of your body to sin, as instruments of wickedness, but rather offer yourself to God, as those who have been brought from death to life; and offer the parts of your body to Him as instruments of righteousness."* You should not use your eyes, hands, feet et cetera, in any way that would serve sin. Whenever you choose to offer yourself to sin, you invite sin to rule in your physical body, which is something God has commanded us not to do. Paul urged,

"You were called to freedom, brethren; only do not turn your freedom into an opportunity for the flesh, but through love serve one another" (Galatians 5:13).

Fame, like flame, is harmless until you start inhaling it. Our most vulnerable point of temptation, pleasure, represents the desire to be sensually satisfied no matter the cost. It may be as harmless as an amusement. Temptation comes to everyone. If temptation can come to the King of kings and Lord of lords, the One who has all authority on heaven and on earth, then it can come to you and me too! By resisting temptation out in the open, we cultivate character down inside. If temptation can destroy pastors and leaders, if temptation can wreck and ruin the work that God wills to do in a person's life, then we bettor be on our guard. Every temptation of satan is anti-God. It seeks to destroy our relationship with Him and our fellowship with His people.

Temptation brings the spectrum of humanity to ground level. The rich and the poor, the presidents, the educated, and the illiterate are all confronted by temptations. There is no safeguard, no preventive measure to take. The devil can attack any one at any level. Our only hope is in the knowledge that when it does come, we can claim victory and become conquerors through Jesus Christ our Lord.

Testing or Temptations?

It is very important to distinguish between temptation and testing. Both are mentioned in scripture and they are very different. Temptation from satan is evil in intent, and it leads to spiritual death. On the other hand, testing is of God for the purpose of spiritual growth and an enduring faith. To distinguish real temptation when it comes your way, ask the simple question: "Does this thought, this attitude, hinder my walk with the Lord? Does it distract me from doing God's will?" If the answer is "Yes," then that's temptation, and you and I must run from it.

Temptation Keeps Coming

"When the devil had finished tempting Jesus, he left Him until an opportune time."

Jesus had won round one, but the fight continued. Satan is a crafty and cunning personality. He knows when to attack us. When do you think he came to Jesus again? Maybe he came some days later when Jesus retuned home to Nazareth and tried to begin his ministry. He started troubling Jesus when He started his public ministry. Luke 4:28-30 tells of His rejection and of how He was run out of town. The heavens rejoiced but not the townspeople; they asked him to leave. May be he was present there when Jesus talked to his disciples about dying. Peter said,

"God forbid that this shall ever happen to you." Jesus replied, "Get behind me, satan. You are a stumbling block to me" (see Matt. 16:22-23).

He was very much there on the night when Peter denied the Lord three times. Here, one of his closest followers quickly claimed that he did not even know the Man, and started cursing the Lord. Maybe Jesus heard his voice, "Do not do it" while praying in the garden. Jesus said, *"Not my will but Thine."* Even on the cross Jesus might have heard the devil's voice prompting Him to step down from the cross and put an end to his pain. But Jesus was victorious over all these temptations. Temptation came throughout the course of Jesus' life on earth.

Trials or Temptations?

There is a definite difference between trials and temptations. Trials are tests of our faith. Normally, there is nothing immoral involved in experiencing a trial. A trial is a hardship the Lord allows us to experience. However, it is generally not something that is evil or brought about by evil.

James addresses the problem of trials in chapter 1 up to verse 12. But in verse 13 he speaks about temptation. Take, for example, Job's trials. He lost his health, his family, his home, his business - he lost everything! But nothing immoral brought about Job's problems. It was a severe series of tests. Or look at a depressed Elijah under the juniper tree. When his life was threatened, he went away to hide and pleaded with God. Nothing immoral or evil on Elijah's part caused him to experience depression. It was a test, a hardship, and an ordeal.

John (the author of Revelation) was banished to the isle of Patmos, but not for moral wrongdoing. Being removed from all that was close and dear to him was his test. But when we consider temptation, it is different from a trial. That is why James includes the word "tempted" in verse 13. Although it is the same Greek word we have read in verses 1 through 12, in his mind it is something different. It changed from the idea of an ordeal to the idea of soliciting evil.

Chapter 5
Joseph's Victory Over Temptation

Abraham's grandson, Jacob, had 12 sons. Joseph, the eleventh son of Jacob, was his favorite because he was the son born in his old age and since he was the son of his favorite wife. When he was 17 years old, he set his 11 brothers against him by telling them his dream of their bowing down to him. Being jealous of Joseph, his brothers dumped him in a pit and sold him as a slave to a caravan of Ishmaelite merchants, who took him to Egypt. Never expecting to see him again, they reported to their father that a wild animal had devoured Joseph (see Gen. 37:33).

Joseph was Vulnerable but Victorious

The Ishmaelite merchants took Joseph to Egypt and sold him as a slave to Potiphar (see Gen. 37:36). Potiphar was an Egyptian and the captain of Pharaoh's guard. He recognized that Joseph was no ordinary man, that the Lord was with him and that the Lord gave him success in everything he did. Not only did Joseph prosper in all that he did, but also the Lord blessed Potiphar's household because of Joseph. In fact, the blessing of the Lord was on everything Potiphar had, both in the house and in the field. Because of this, Potiphar eventually promoted Joseph to a high position (see Gen. 39:3-5).

Potiphar's wife, noticing that Joseph was well-built and handsome, attempted to seduce him and said to him, "Lie with me." But Joseph did not yield to her request (see Gen. 39:7-8). Joseph was in a very vulnerable situation that would have caused most young men to yield to temptation for the following reasons:

a. From his life situation we see that Joseph had very little opportunity for physical, or even social contact with the opposite sex.

b. The woman was persistent. *"She spoke to Joseph day after day, [but] he did not listen to her [request] to lie beside her, or be with her"* (Gen. 39:10).

c. Potiphar's wife could create complex problems for Joseph if he refused her. In fact, pleasing a woman of her position might have helped Joseph to get new promotions in his position in Egypt.

d. Joseph was away from his family and probably felt lonely and homesick at times. An invitation to any kind of companionship must have been attractive.

e. It was unlikely that anyone would have known. The only thing that keeps some people from sin is the fear that others will find out. Joseph had nothing to loose; he was an insignificant slave. This was his one chance for a little pleasure. In spite of such vulnerability, he maintained his moral purity. "Purity in your heart produces power in your life."

Joseph's Three Reasons for Rejecting the Offer

Joseph simply said no to the offer and gave Potiphar's wife three reasons for his refusal. The first reason was regarding his *relationship with man.* Joseph saw the seriousness of violating the trust his master had in him. He refused and said to his master's wife,

"B*ehold, with me here, my master does not concern himself with anything in the house, and he has put all that he owns in my charge"* (Gen. 39:8).

The second reason, Joseph would not lie with Potiphar's wife was regarding his respect for the marriage relationship. He said to her,

"There is no one greater in this house than I, and he has withheld nothing from me except you, because you are his wife. How then could I do this great evil and sin against God" (Gen. 39:9)?

He did not want to separate what God had joined together (see Mk. 10:9).

The third reason was regarding his relationship with God. Since Joseph maintained a close relationship with God, he was able to remain blameless in his moral relationship with Potiphar and his wife. He obviously valued his relationship with the Lord more than personal gratification. Without God in the picture, human relationships can be influenced entirely through emotional attractions.

The Strength Of Joseph's Character

To have sinned with Potiphar's wife would have been to sin against God. Only after King David committed adultery with Bathsheba did he realize that he had sinned against God (see Ps. 51:4). As for Joseph, beyond the face of the adulterous seductress, he saw another face (God's) full of grace and loveliness, which he dared not hurt or displease. The fact that Joseph could resist the same temptation many times reveals the strength of his character. To be in the presence of Potiphar's wife was like being in the presence of temptation for Joseph, which is why he avoided her. It is wise to keep away from sources of temptation. Once when none of Potiphar's servants were inside, she caught him by his cloak, but Joseph ran out of the house. Perhaps she was looking for such an opportunity so that there may be no eyewitnesses. The most important step Joseph took to resist temptation was to run away from it. Paul says, "Now flee from youthful lusts..." (2 Tim. 2:22). Running from a sinful situation is not a cowardly act. It is the right thing to do. Through Joseph's example, we learn that in spite of the allure of temptation, sin can be avoided.

Satan enters every Eden. He came to tempt Joseph, not in the form of a serpent but in the form of a beautiful woman. Temptation is all around us. Our eyes, ears, and emotions are constantly bombarded with immorality. Sexual sin is not the only form of temptation. Some feel strongly tempted toward other sins like covetousness, pride, lying, et cetera. Our consumer-oriented society encourages greed. On the streets we pass through filthy cinema posters and advertisements. Much of the radio and television programs glorify rebellion, drug abuse, and sexual perversion. The world says, "There are no absolutes; right and wrong change with the times; the past is past and the present is present." It is true that times have changed, and that we are now living in an experience-oriented society; but we cannot forsake godly principles on which our families will operate. Otherwise, soon our rules will be mixed with the rules of the world, and our daughters and sons will not know the difference.

We know from Romans that the people decided to exchange the truth of God for a lie, and worshiped and served the creature rather than the Creator (see Rom. 1:25). But, simply deciding to change the truth didn't change it. Deciding to believe that a loaded gun will not kill us if we put it to our head and pull the trigger will not change the fact that it will! God has set within each of us a conscience that bears witness with our spirits. The law of God is written in our hearts, which tell us when we have crossed over the fence into immorality (see Rom. 2:15). The Bible tells us that there are times when the right feeling can lead to the wrong actions. *"There is a way which seems right to a man, but its end is the way of death"* (Prov. 14:12).

We must avoid nurturing relationships that influence our potential lustful passions, just as Joseph avoided Potiphar's wife. Rather, we must be occupied with what God has placed before us to do. We must also remember that Joseph's experience was both a temptation and a trial. This is difficult to comprehend, for it is satan, not God, who tempts (see Jas. 1:13). God often allows trials in our lives so that we might grow spiritually, which prepares us for greater responsibility in

His kingdom (see 1 Pet. 1:6-7). God can actually take evil (caused by satan) and make it work for our good (see Rom. 8:28)!

The greatest temptation we all face when someone mistreats us is to seek revenge. Joseph had to face that temptation also. In doing so, Joseph was not "overcome by evil." Instead, he "overcame evil with good" (see Rom. 12:21). How did Joseph overcome this temptation? What held him back from falling into temptation? It was not because he was afraid of Potiphar, nor was it because this beautiful woman did not attract him. He resisted the temptation because he feared God and would not do anything to displease him. Joseph won the battle because he learned to say the hardest little word, "No." He is a great example of a young man who possessed many ideal characteristics. David had the same kind of temptation that Joseph had, but in a moment of time he forgot God and yielded to temptation.

The most important motivating source for not yielding to temptation should be our relationship with God. As Paul stated to Titus, *"For the grace of God has appeared, bringing salvation to all men, instructing us to deny ungodliness and worldly desires and to live sensibly, righteously and godly in the present age..."* (Titus 2:11-12). We access such grace through a committed relationship with God.

The Lord Was With Him

When Joseph ran out of the house, the woman concocted a story designed to slander Joseph. This reminds us that doing what is right is no guarantee that everything will turn out right. In a fallen world, sometimes a holy and honest life puts us in conflict with corrupt society. We may be persecuted because we do not fit in, but God rewards those who walk uprightly (see Jn. 15:18-21). Joseph was successful because the Lord was with him (see Gen. 39:21).

The presence of God makes all the difference. When Gideon protested that he was unable to deliver the Israelites from the Midianites, God said, *"I will be with you"* (Judg. 6:16). When Jeremiah complained that he was too young to serve as a prophet, God said,

"I am with you" (Jer. 1:8). Jesus also promised that he would always be with us (see Matt. 28:20). A lie was told against Joseph and he was imprisoned, but God was with him. Whatever Joseph did, the Lord caused him to prosper (see Gen. 39:23).

In the course of time, Joseph was released from prison and God made him a prominent official in the land. Perhaps this incident was allowed by God to test Joseph (see Ps. 105:17-19). Joseph's uncompromising position of moral purity cost him something. He was sent to prison because he refused to succumb to the seductions of Potiphar's wife, who, out of wrath, retaliated against Joseph by lying about him. Joseph's life story demonstrates clearly that, at times, God allows suffering in the lives of His children to accomplish His own special purposes.

Job is a classic illustration of one who suffered. His situation, though much different from Joseph's, also has some similarities. In Job's and Joseph's lives, God had special purposes for allowing them to suffer. With Job, it was an unusual demonstration to satan and us that, though we do not understand why we are suffering, we can believe and trust God and remain true to Him no matter what the circumstances are. For Joseph, it was to prepare him for a greater task that had both earthly and eternal implications.

In every instance, God allows the righteous to suffer in order to use them in a special way. He will certainly make them stronger and more effective following the trial. This indeed is why God allows suffering in the first place. Yet because Joseph obeyed Him, God turned the situation around and prospered Joseph in the prison. God used this experience as a gateway to future blessing. Joseph learned to trust and obey God in life's hard places. He learned that moral purity, although costly, is the pathway to power and great blessing.

Joseph Never Lost His Vision In The Face Of Opposition

The first test in his life was his being thrown into the pit (see Gen. 37:24). There was no way that Joseph could see the throne from the pit. However, he never lost his vision. You should never loose your vision in the face of opposition. The second test dealt with his ability to resist temptation. Some times you may say "yes" to God, but do you also say "no" to the devil (see Gen. 39:7-12)? Joseph was thrown into the prison because of false accusation. Likewise, our vision can be tested by false accusation. When Stephen got accused, his vision did not get dimmer but grew stronger and brighter until he was even able to see the Lord (see Acts 7: 55).

Remaining true to God-given vision can keep us from sin, as we see in Joseph's life. Joseph was faithful to the vision God had given him and was therefore also faithful and loyal in his relationships (see Gen. 37:5-10). Remaining faithful to God's vision causes us to find favor with God, with others, and to be successful in our endeavors (see Gen. 39:4,21). Your patient faith will serve as a witness to those who may have scoffed while you waited for the vision's fulfillment.

As Joseph discovered, sometimes it takes many years to see the fulfillment of a vision that was received early in life. Waiting patiently is not always easy, especially in the face of adversity. Staying true to God's vision for your life will keep you faithful to Him in all you do, restraining you from compromise and sin (see Gen. 39:9). The story of Joseph teaches us that great wisdom and discernment must be exercised in sharing with others the visions that God has given us individually.

He Waited For God's Vindication

Some of us have faced the same kind of mistreatment that Joseph faced. No matter what the emotional or physical pain, we must not allow ourselves to become bitter towards God, for if we do, we would only compound our problems. Not that God will turn against us; He never will. His love is unconditional. But if we are angry towards God, then in that state of mind we may be violating all the necessary steps that it takes to draw on Him as our divine source of strength and help. Joseph patiently waited for God to vindicate him, and to honor both his faith and his positive attitudes. So should we! Waiting eleven long years in prison must have been the most difficult thing Joseph had to do.

While in prison, Joseph interpreted the dreams of the king's chief cupbearer and the chief baker. When Joseph interpreted the cupbearer's dream, reassuring him that he would be reinstated to his former position, he asked this high-ranking official to put in a good word for him to the king. This must have been Joseph's first ray of hope for release since his confinement to prison by Potiphar, several years before. Every day he must have waited for some word, or some indication that Pharaoh was concerned about his plight. After all, if the cupbearer had told the whole story, Pharaoh would have known that Joseph's God had enabled him to interpret dreams accurately. Surely Pharaoh would be interested in discovering more about Joseph's ability. But no word came. Days turned into weeks, which turned into months, which turned into "two full years!" It was thirteen years that he had been in prison, paying the price for endeavoring to live a holy life. Nonetheless, Joseph waited patiently for God to set the record straight.

We must remember that God had not revealed to Joseph what was going to happen. The fact that the Lord gave him the supernatural ability to predict someone else's future did not mean that he could predict his own. Joseph had to continue his prison experience by faith, continuing to hope that God would make it possible for him to be released.

Joseph knew he was innocent and he also knew that this was the time to express it. I'm glad he did, for we know that there's a time to defend oneself against false accusation, even though God is the ultimate vindicator. There's also a time to ask someone to put in a good word for us even though we are trusting God with all our heart to help and defend us. But it must be emphasized that timing is very important. Let's think for a moment about Joseph's family relationship. He probably wanted to return to his family in Canaan (see Gen. 40:15). It had been thirteen long years since he had seen his father. Furthermore, since Joseph was a sensitive man, he must have grieved deeply for his father, who had believed that Joseph was devoured by a wild animal.

Fortunately, Joseph had hope beyond hope. That's what kept him from despair during this terrible ordeal. His hope was neither in Potiphar, nor in the cupbearer, nor even in the King of Egypt, but was ultimately in God. Although men failed him, he knew God was still with him in the prison.

One of the great virtues God was developing in Joseph's life was patience, which is the essence of learning to wait. We read that the chief cupbearer did not remember Joseph. The historical record continues, "When two full years had passed, Pharaoh had a dream" (see Gen. 40:23; 41:1).

Eventually, when Pharaoh heard about Joseph, he was impressed, and sent word for him. Pharaoh said,

"...I have heard it said of you, that when you hear a dream you can interpret it."

Joseph took absolutely no credit, telling Pharaoh that he could interpret his dreams, but that God would give the answer Pharaoh desires (see Gen. 41:14-16). Pharaoh related his two dreams to Joseph, and Joseph was able to give instant interpretations (see Gen. 41:17-32). Through this dream, God was warning Pharaoh of the coming seven years of famine after the seven years of abundance. Not only did Joseph give an interpretation of the dream, but he also made a very wise proposal. He suggested that Pharaoh look for a discerning and wise man, someone he could put in charge of the land of Egypt. He further suggested a plan for storing up food during the seven years of abundance, which in turn could be used and distributed during the seven years of famine. Pharaoh's response to Joseph's plan was positive. He asked his officials,

"Can we find anyone like this man, in whom is a divine spirit?" (see Gen. 41:33-36).

Pharaoh knew that Joseph's capabilities were from God. Furthermore, he now saw him against the backdrop of all the other magicians and wise men of Egypt.

Proper reasoning would help us understand why God allowed this to happen. Had Joseph come to Pharaoh two years before, it would have probably been only because of the king's curiosity. There would have been no personal need. Consequently, there would have been no opportunity for Pharaoh to compare Joseph's success with the failure of the Egyptian wise men. The thoroughness with which Pharaoh tried to determine the meaning of his dreams is seen in his conclusion:

"There is no one so discerning and wise as you." (Gen. 41:39).

Had Joseph attempted to vindicate himself in his own efforts rather than waiting for God's moment in his life, he may never have had the unique opportunity the Lord brought his way that day. Wrong timing often causes legitimate self-defense to appear defensive.

Joseph went from the "prison" to the "palace"- not only to live there, but also to have authority over the whole kingdom of Egypt. Thus Pharaoh says,

"You shall be over my house...only in the throne I will be greater than you." (Gen. 41:40).

Joseph became the grand vizier of Egypt. All of Joseph's patient waiting, faithful efforts, and positive attitudes over the past thirteen years did not go waste. Waiting time is not wasting time. A period of waiting often allows time for one's true character to be developed and revealed.

Joseph would have understood God's supernatural purposes as he progressed through these painful experiences spanning thirteen years. God's divine pattern for his life must have come into focus rather suddenly when he was promoted so quickly and so dramatically. Seldom does any person who is a foreigner, recently released from prison, even when innocent, suddenly become a primary ruler of the most significant and affluent kingdom in the world. The privileges, power, and prestige that went with this promotion accentuate why this event is so dramatic and miraculous.

God was preparing Joseph to endure difficult and demanding circumstances. There is a price to be paid for every leadership position. Some will become jealous. There will be rumors and false accusations. There will be misunderstandings and miscommunications. There will be sleepless nights and unending problems. Samuel Rutherford once stated that we should praise God for the hammer, the file, and the furnace. He goes on to explain that the hammer moulds us, the file shapes us, and the fire tempers us. All three experiences are painful, but we can praise God for them because we know and love God who wields them.

Pharaoh gave Joseph an Egyptian name and married him into a prominent Egyptian family. However, Joseph gave his own sons Hebrew names, a practice that suggests he maintained his own identity. Thus, through Joseph's example, we recognize the elements of a noble character-piety, pure and high morality, simplicity, gentleness, fidelity, patience, perseverance, an iron will, and an indomitable energy.

God was preparing Joseph for future difficult and demanding circumstances. There is a price to be paid for every leadership position. Some will become jealous. There will be rumors and false accusations. There will be misunderstandings and miscommunications. There will be sleepless nights and unending problems. Samuel Rutherford once stated that we should praise God for the hammer, the file, and the furnace. He goes on to explain that the hammer moulds us, the file sharpens us, and the fire tempers us. All three experiences are painful, but we can praise God for them because we know and love God who wields them.

Pharaoh gave Joseph an Egyptian name and married him into a prominent Egyptian family. However, Joseph gave his two sons Hebrew names, a practice that suggests he maintained his own identity. Thus, through Joseph's examples, we recognize the elements of a noble character: piety, pure and high morality, simplicity, gentleness, fidelity, patience, perseverance, fortitude, and an indomitable energy.

Chapter 6
Jesus' Victory Over Temptation

Jesus was tempted in everything exactly as we are and "yet was without sin" (see Heb. 4:15). He resisted temptation by subjecting Himself to the Spirit's power rather than by relying upon his capabilities as a human being (see Luke 4:1). In fact, His ministry was performed totally under the power of the Holy Spirit of God. Jesus overcame His temptations over the world (see 1 Jn. 5:4), over the flesh (see Gal 5:16), and over the enemy (see Eph. 6:11,13).

Through The Word Of God

Jesus was led by the Spirit into the desert to be tempted by the devil. After fasting forty days and forty nights, He was hungry (see Matt. 4:1-2). During this temptation, He defeated Satan each time by using the Word of God. The Psalmist says,

"Thy word have I hid in mine heart, that I might not sin against thee" (Psalm 119:11).

Let us review the previous comparisons made between Jesus' temptation in Luke 4:1-13 and 1 John 2:16:

Luke 4:1-13	**1 John 2:16**
Stones to bread	"Lust of the flesh"

Kingdoms of the earth	"Lust of the eyes"
Pinnacle of the temple	"Pride of life"

Satan tried to use the "lust of the flesh" against Jesus. He tempted Jesus to use His power to convert the stones into bread and satisfy His hunger. This passage shows us a personal devil. The devil is not merely a force or an influence, but a person. The devil tempts people to do evil and accuses them before God (see Job 1:6-12; 2:1-6). Jesus was tempted in every part of His humanity, as we are. Satan was trying to make Jesus selfish, greedy, and impatient just for a moment. He said to Him,

"If you are God's Son, order this stone to turn into bread." Jesus answered, "The Scripture says: Man cannot live by bread alone."

Jesus was implying that he came to fill the hungry that needed more than bread. They need the Bread of Life, which is the Word of God. Then the devil took him up and showed him all the kingdoms of the world, and said,

"I will give you all this power and all this wealth... if you worship me." Jesus answered, "The scripture says, worship the Lord your God and serve only him." (see Matt. 4:10).

In other words Jesus was saying, "If I am God's Son I must do things God's way, and His way is different from yours. I bow to one person only and He is God."

The devil then took Him to Jerusalem and set Him on the highest point of the temple, and said to Him, *"If you are God's Son, throw yourself down from here...."* Jesus answered, "The scripture says, do not put the Lord your God to the test." In other words, Jesus knew that God wouldn't let Him down, so there was no need to prove Himself. Faith does not ask for proof. With God there are no stunts, short cuts or cheap tricks. Satan wanted Jesus to draw on His divine power to meet His need instead of submitting to the will of God for His life. Jesus, however, demonstrated something far more important. Rather than showing He had the power to change rocks into bread, He showed

He was committed to God's will. We can observe that His commitment grew out of His understanding of Scripture. Jesus not only knew the Scriptures, but He also knew how to apply them to specific situations.

God's Word is a powerful weapon, but in order for that weapon to be effective in your encounter with satan and his demons, there are two basic requirements:

1. familiarity with the weapon, and
2. using the weapon in the power of the Spirit.

Be familiar with your weapon. When a soldier goes into basic training he is given a rifle. That weapon becomes his closest companion. He eats and sleeps with it. He must be able to take it apart and put it together again blindfolded. Similarly, you must be familiar with Scripture. Take every opportunity to learn all you can through the instruction of others and from your own private reading and meditation. When satan confronts you with a specific temptation, use God's Word in the power of the Holy Spirit.

Through His Life, Death And Resurrection

Faith, in the Person and work of Christ, releases the Christian from the power and dominion that sin had over him (see Rom. 8:9). He is now free to choose to walk in obedience to God (see Rom. 6:8-14). Faith forms a battle line against every form of evil. Faith finds the strength to be an overcomer of temptation. While it is Christ who succors and delivers in temptation, the will of the sanctified is in perfect harmony with the Holy nature of Jesus. The modern conception of a holy life, mixed with sin, worldliness, and carnal promptings and actions is not only unscriptural, but is also opposed to God and His holiness. In Him is no variation, neither shadow of turning.

For what the law was powerless to do in that it was weakened by the sinful nature, God did by sending His own Son in the likeness of sinful man... in order that the righteous requirements of the law might be fully met in us, who do not live according to the sinful nature [flesh] but according to the spirit (Rom. 8:3-4).

As Christians, we are called to live in victory! Through Christ, this victory is ours. We recognize Jesus as divine, but He was also human like any one of us. He was a young man when these temptations occurred. These tests were not haphazard or random. They were an organized and systematic attack on every aspect of Jesus' life and career.

The tempter directed his first test at the physical condition of our Lord. Satan attacked when Jesus was hungry and likely exhausted. In the first temptation, the devil challenged Jesus as the Son of God. It was a temptation of a private nature. Cleverly, the devil uses Jesus' deity as leverage to ply Him into acting independently of His Father. He tried to destroy Jesus by drawing Him away from His Father and His mission. Temptation is not sin, for Christ was tempted as we are, yet remained sinless (see Heb. 4:15; Mt. 4:1; Lk.22:28). Temptation becomes sin only when you yield to the suggestion of evil. Satan also tempts us to forsake God's purpose for our lives. He will try to get us to use our God-given gifts for selfish ends rather than in committed service for God.

The second temptation of Jesus appealed to the desire for personal gain and glory. Having failed to lure Christ with self-gratification, the devil attempts to catch Him with the offer of power. It wasn't about physical needs. Jesus knew that Psalm 91 is a call for God's people to trust that He takes care of them. Jesus then quoted Deuteronomy 6:16 to show the error of trying to back God into a corner and force Him to do something. A correct understanding of God's Word will help us know when someone is misapplying it. Satan casts doubt on what God has said to us in the Scripture. He challenges our understanding of God's Word. Hence, it is necessary to know for ourselves what the Scripture says.

In the third test in the wilderness, satan again attacks the spiritual life of Jesus. This attack was public. Satan sought to get Jesus to turn away from his role as the suffering Servant. Jesus would not turn to worship anyone or anything other than God. The reason He gave is based on the clear teaching of Scripture (see Deut. 6:13). He ordered satan to stop trying to get him to turn away from the Father. With this, satan left and the angels came to attend Jesus (see Matt. 4:11). When we reject satan's offer, then the angels come to minister to us.

Perhaps you say that the devil makes you to do certain things. Actually, the devil can't make you do anything. He may be cleverly preparing the way and would lay the bait. He takes note of your habits, and observes your hangouts. Then he prepares a lure, tailor-made for your weakness, and drops it right in front of your nose. The choice is yours. After laying the bait, he gives the appeal. He can't make you bite, but he knows what happens inside when you we catch a glimpse of that tantalizing bait. Your fleshly nature draws you to it. You linger over it, play around it and fantasize about it in your mind until it consumes your imagination. Now your real struggle begins. Immediately, your conscience warns you regarding the danger. You know it's wrong to bite the bait. You may even feel the barbed consequences starting to poke through the bait. But Satan's invitation looks so delicious and you may take a mouth full till you realize the pain of the hook in your cheek. It may be too late to come out of it because you are already hooked. Always there is a way out, but you may still have to endure the consequences.

If Jesus had jumped off the pinnacle, His life would most likely have been preserved, but not His mission. The rest was to see whether He would draw all people to Himself by relying on the way of sensationalism or the way of the cross. Jesus chose the cross. No matter how cleverly and smoothly the devil paved the way, Jesus would not be enticed to abandon God's narrow, difficult way.

And when the devil had finished every temptation, he departed from him until an opportune time (see Matt. 4:11,13). Satan retreats, but only temporarily. When he leaves, count on another attack. Satan is never discouraged by defeat. He keeps trying again and again. Directly after Christ was declared to be the Son of God and the Savior of the world, He was tempted. Great privileges and special tokens of divine favor will not secure any from being tempted. However, the

Holy Spirit testifies to our being adopted as children of God, which answers all the suggestions that the evil spirit uses to tempt us. Commenting on this character of the devil, Martin Luther said,

"The devil takes no holiday; he never rests. If beaten, he rises again. If he cannot enter in front, he steals in at the rear. If he cannot enter in the rear, he breaks through the roof or enters by tunneling under the threshold. He labors until he is in. He uses great cunning and many a plan. When one miscarries, he has another at hand and continues his attempts until he wins."

Satan's temptations are very creative. If one doesn't work, he can always pull five more out of his hat.

Leander S. Keyser has suggested that temptation can come to man along only three avenues. All other temptations are merely variants of these three.

Appetite: The desire to enjoy things (see Mt. 4:2-4; Lk. 4:2-4). In his first letter, John refers to this as *"the lust of the flesh"* (see 1 Jn. 2:16). Since Jesus was hungry, Satan made his first approach on the physical plane and in the realm of legitimate appetite. He came in the role of a benefactor.

Ambition: The desire to achieve things (see Mt. 4:5-6; Lk. 4:9-11. This John designates *"the pride of life"* (see 1 Jn. 2:16).

Avarice: The desire to obtain things (see Mt. 4:8-11; Lk.4:5-7) is designated by John as *"the lust of the eyes"* (see 1 Jn. 2:16).

The Mathew Henry commentary says:

"In the temptation of Christ it appears that our enemy is subtle, spiteful, and very daring; but he can be resisted. It is a comfort to us that Christ suffered, being tempted; for thus it appears that our temptations, if not yielded to, are not sins, they are afflictions only. Satan aimed in all his temptations, to bring Christ to sin against God."

1.) He tempted Him to despair of His Father's goodness, and to distrust His Father's care for Him. It is one of the wiles of Satan to take advantage of our outward condition; and those who are brought into straits have need to double their guard.

2.) Satan tempted Christ to presume upon his Father's power and protection, in a point of safety. Nor are any extremes more dangerous than despair and presumption, especially in the affairs of our souls. Satan has no objection to holy places as the scene of his assaults. Let us not, in any place, forget to keep watch. The holy city is the place, where he does, with the greatest advantage, tempt men with pride and presumption. All high places are slippery places. Advancements in the world are targets for satan to shoot his fiery darts at.

3.) Satan tempted Christ with idolatry by offering Him the kingdoms of the world and their glory. The glory of the world is the most charming temptation to the unthinking and unwary. Christ was tempted to worship satan. He rejected the proposal with abhorrence - "Get thee hence, Satan!" Some temptations are openly wicked; and they are not merely to be opposed, but rejected at once. It is good to be quick and firm in resisting temptation. Remember, if we resist the devil, he will flee from us.

Mark notices that, while in the wilderness, Christ is with the wild beasts. This exemplifies how the Father takes care of Him during His testing. God protects us from the wild beasts during our times of testing. The serpent tempted the first Adam in the garden, the Second Adam in the wilderness; with different success indeed; and ever since he still tempts the children of both, in all places and conditions.

Often in such activities as laboring, eating, drinking, praying, and fasting are found the most assaults against one's spirit. However, in them we also accomplish the sweetest victories. The ministry of the good angels is to comfort the tempted, after the malignant designs of the evil angels have run their course. However good such angelic ministration is for us, much more does it comfort us to have the indwelling of the Holy Spirit. (see Mk. 1:12-13).

Darby's Synopsis commentary says:

"It is in the spirit of simple and humble obedience that power lies; for where it exists, Satan can do nothing. God is there, and accordingly the enemy is conquered. These three temptations are addressed to the Lord in the three characters, of man, of Messiah, and of Son of man. He had no sinful desires like fallen man, but He was hungered. The tempter would persuade Him to satisfy this need without God. The promises in the Psalms belonged to Him as being made to the Messiah. And all the kingdoms of the world were His as the Son of man. He always replies as a faithful Israelite, personally responsible to God, making use of the Book of Deuteronomy."

The first temptation was physical, and the second was mental. In the third, satan invades the realm of the spiritual-trying to attain a place that belongs to God alone. The first was the temptation to satisfy a legitimate appetite by illegitimate means. The second was the temptation to bring about spiritual glory by worldly means. The third was the temptation to obtain a lawful heritage by unlawful methods. The record implies that in each case Jesus heard the temptation from within, but did not open the door to the tempter. In this way He gained a stunning victory over His enemy, the benefits of which can be shared today by every tempted soul. Because the Christ, with Whom we are united by faith, was victorious over every class of temptation, we may share in His triumph as we appropriate it by faith.

Chapter 7

Samson Played With His Anointing

Israel was in a desperate need for a deliverer. Samson was the one to deliver them from the oppression of the Philistines. The angel of God promised to Manoah and his wife that they would have a son dedicated to God to be a life-long Nazirite and that, being mightily empowered by the Spirit of God, he would be the deliverer of Israel. Thus Samson was the renowned judge.

How Did The Mighty Samson Fall?

Anyone can fall if his actions are contrary to his basic convictions or moral principles given by God, and if his judgment has been clouded by "desire" or overwhelmed by "passion." Man develops character through his concrete decisions. Our decisions determine our destiny. Circumstances do not make a man; they reveal what he's made of. They set before you a temptation so alluring that in your own strength you will not be able to overcome it. Our trouble is not that we are tempted, but that we don't turn to God for deliverance and turn to someone else for counseling when the temptation is before us.

The same is true in Samson's story. The people of Israel were forever sinning and repenting. The anger of the Lord became hot against Israel so much so that he permitted the people to be vexed and oppressed by heathen kings for eighteen years. As the people cried and repented, God grieved for their misery. Fresh apostasy, however, engulfed Israel, so God delivered them into the hands of the Philistines for forty years. Samson was born at the height of the Philistines' power.

The angel of God appeared to the wife of Manoah and said to her,

Behold now, you are barren and have borne no children, but you shall conceive and give birth to a son... and no razor shall come upon his head, for the boy shall be a Nazirite to God from the womb; and he shall begin to deliver Israel from the hands of the Philistines (Judges 13:3-5).

The woman then went and reported to her husband all that the angel had told her.

Just as the angel had said, a son was born to Manoah and his wife and they named him Samson. He grew up to live a life of a Nazirite. The Nazirites were not supposed to drink wine or eat anything that came from the vine such as raisins and grapes, since the "fruit of the vine" represented earthly joy to the nation of Israel. It was to cheer the heart. However, a Nazirite was not supposed to find his joy in anything on the earth. He was to find his joy only in the things of God. There is no record that Samson ever found his joy in the things of his life! He was always finding his pleasure in the things of this world. The Bible tells us that the joy of the Lord is our strength, our portion.

Second, a Nazirite was not supposed to cut his hair. He had never received a haircut until Delilah gave him one. Why was this necessary? Because the Bible tells us, *"Does not even nature itself teach you that if a man has long hair, it is a dishonor to him, but if a woman has long hair, it is a glory to her? For her hair is given to her for a covering"* (1 Cor. 11:14). The Scripture makes it very clear that long hair dishonors a man. But the Nazirites were expected to be willing to bear the shame for God. He was to be different. John the Baptist was a Nazirite, which explained why no razor touched his head or face.

Third, a Nazirite was not supposed to come near a dead body. When a loved one died, he was not to go to the funeral or have anything to do with it. In other words, he had to put God first, above his relatives and loved ones. Samson gave a fresh start to the humiliated and depressed condition of the people of Israel. He was appointed by God to deal with the existing emergency. Self-denial should have reached its highest significance in his life. He should have been a living example of Israel's calling as a consecrated people. Although he judged Israel for twenty years, he did not have a fitting personal character. Samson took advantage of his special endowment, thinking his special gift enabled him to accomplish extraordinary deeds. He yielded to fleshly sins and personal gratification.

Samson, the mighty strong man, is not remembered for his great victories, but rather for his fall. God called Samson to defeat Israel's enemies, but a woman named Delilah robbed him of his strength. Samson's story warns us that we can lose God's anointing if we are not responsible with it. In spite of his spiritual and moral decline, God continued to give him the gift of supernatural strength. Considering the life he lived, he was given more space than any other judge, because, of all the judges, Samson was the only Nazirite.

The Secret of Samson's Strength

Strength is the first thing we think of when we think of Samson. He was a physical giant but a moral weakling. His whole life was a scene of follies and sin. He mastered others, but he could not master himself. Samson could not be defeated by anyone as long as he had his long hair, and as long as he was under the anointing of God. The Bible says that the spirit of God would move on Samson and he would rise up and accomplish feats with supernatural power (see Judg. 13:25; 14:6). But Samson had a weakness: He loved the world and what it offered him. He wanted the very thing his vows prohibited.

Samson had seen a beautiful girl in Timnah, one of the daughters of the Philistines. He wanted her as his wife. As a Nazarite, he was not supposed to marry anyone from the pagan culture. Since the woman looked good to him, he insisted that he have her (see Judg. 14:1-3). Samson then went down to Timnah with his father and mother. When they came as far as the vineyards of Timnah, a young lion came roaring toward them. When the Spirit of the Lord came upon Samson, he tore the lion as one tears a kid, though he had nothing in his hand (see Judg. 14:5-6). While in Timnah, Samson proposed a riddle to the thirty companions who were with him. He gave them seven days to answer his riddle. At the end of seven days, through Samson's wife, the men were able to get the answer to the riddle. Then the Spirit of the Lord came upon him and he went down to Ashkelon and killed thirty of them and took their spoil, and gave the changes of clothes to those who had told him the riddle (see Judg. 14:12-19). The marriage ended in a matter of days and resulted in the death of many people.

On another occasion, when Samson felt that the Philistines had mistreated him, he caught three hundred foxes, tied them in pairs, tail to tail, and placed a torch between each pair. When he had set fire to the torches, he released the foxes into the standing grain of the Philistines, burning up both the stocks and the standing grain, along with the vineyard and groves (see Judg. 15:4-5). He then went and lived in the cleft of the rock of Etam. The Philistines marched against Judah to take revenge on Samson. The men of Judah went down to the cleft of Etam to take Samson and hand him over to the Philistines. This is the time when Samson first began to play with God's anointing. He considered himself invincible, and allowed the Israelites to tie him up and hand him over to the Philistines. They bound him with two new ropes and brought him up from the rock. When the Philistines met them at Lehi, the Spirit of the Lord came upon Samson so mightily that the ropes that were on his arms were as flax that is burned with fire and his bonds dropped from his hands. Samson found a fresh donkey jawbone and used it to kill a thousand Philistine men (see Judg. 15:9-15). He thought he was mocking his enemies, but actually he was setting himself up for his downfall. Samson had a great anointing, but he came to a place in his life where he thought he could do all that he wanted and get away with it. Today, many men of God are in that same place. They are very much under the mighty anointing and have a wonderful ministry with signs and wonders. Because of the signs, wonders, and miracles, they begin to think they can do anything they want.

Shortly after the incident in the Philistine camp, Samson again chose to toy with the anointing. Scripture says that he went to Gaza, where he saw a harlot, and went in to her. When the Gazites knew that Samson was there, they surrounded the place and lay in wait for him all night at the gate of the city, planning to kill him early in the morning.

Now Samson lay until midnight, [then] he arose and took hold of the doors of the city gate and the two posts and pulled them up along with the bars; [and] he put them on his shoulders and carried them up to the top of the mountain which is opposite Hebron (Judg. 16:1-3).

Where did he get all his strength? His strength was not in his arms, although he killed a thousand Philistines at one time with them. His strength was not in his back, although he carried the gates of Gaza. Samson's real strength was not even in his hair, although he was weak when it was cut. His strength was from God. In each instance we see that the Spirit of the Lord came upon him. If God had not intervened each time, he would have been as any other man.

Samson is forever recorded in our memories as the man who relinquished his anointing for the love of an adulterous woman. Samson, the mighty strongman is not remembered for his great victories, but rather for his fall. God called Samson to defeat Israel's enemies, but a woman named Delilah robbed him of his strength. Samson's story warns us that if we play with God's anointing we can loose it.

The Cause of Samson's Weakness

Samson, the strongest man of his generation, was tragically unable to control his lust. First, he fell for the woman at Timnah. He then went into a harlot at Gaza. Delilah was the third woman with whom he sinned. When thousands of men had failed to overcome Samson, a wheedling woman succeeded. Desire was his only ruler.

The Philistines came to Delilah with a proposition,

"Entice him, and see where his great strength lies and how we may overpower him that we may bind him to afflict him. Then we will each give you eleven hundred pieces of silver" (Judg. 16:5).

Delilah was not a woman of character and was not faithful to Samson. She said to him, *"Please tell me where your great strength is and how you may be bound to afflict you"* (Judg. 16:6). Samson told her if they bound him with seven fresh cords that have not been dried, then he shall become weak and be like any other man. She bound him with the seven fresh cords that the Philistines had given her and she cried, *"The Philistines are upon you, Samson!"* However, he snapped the cords as a fire would break a slender thread (see Judg. 16:9). Delilah tried again. *"Behold, you have deceived me and told me lies; now please tell me, how you may be bound?" He told her, "If they bind me tightly with new ropes which have not been used, then I shall become weak and be like any other man."* Again when she cried out, he rose up and broke the ropes like you would a thin string (see Judg. 16:10-12).

Rather than seeing Delilah as a viable threat, Samson took God's anointing for granted. The key to his anointing was still a secret. But Delilah didn't back down. The next time she tried to coax Samson to reveal the key to his anointing, he came closer to telling her the secret. He even mentioned part of the secret: his hair. She said, *"So far, you have done nothing but lie to me, so, please tell me, how you may be bound"* (see Judg.16:13)? The devil will come to us constantly, trying to find the key to the anointing on our lives - just as Delilah did with Samson. Samson said, *"If you weave the seven locks of my hair with the web and fasten it with a pin then I shall become weak and be like any other man"* (Judg. 16:13). She did this and the same thing happened. He again came out as strong as ever.

Samson had played with Delilah on the previous occasions, but now he was starting to touch the very source of God's anointing on his life. *"It came about when she pressed him daily with her words and urged him, that his soul was annoyed to death"* (Judg. 16:16). That's what satan wants to do. He wants to wear us down. He wants to get us to a place where we act upon our hearts and compromise the deep things of God. Finally, Samson broke down. He told Delilah all that was in his heart. He said, *"A razor has never come on my head, for I have been a Nazirite to God from my mother's womb. If I am shaved, then my strength will leave me, and I shall become weak and be like any other man"* (Judg. 16:17). Samson said that his strength was in his hair. This shows that he merely depended on his anointing. If he had said that his strength was in his God, he would have never fallen. Our anointing or spiritual gifts cannot take us to heaven, but only our obedience to the will and the word of God.

Samson had begun to think that even if they shave his hair, he would be invincible. But he had lost the anointing. There are people in churches today who have lost the anointing and don't know it. Some of them are even deacons, elders, and pastors. In the end, Samson was captured by the Philistines and his eyes gouged out. He was then taken to Gaza, bound with bronze chains, and was put as a grinder in the prison.

The lure of sexual fantasy can begin like the wisp of a wind, but it will eventually tear through your life like a tornado, devastating everything and everyone in sight. Satan attacks the individual Christian, mostly through temptation. First of all, he will seek to tempt a believer to become absorbed into the world's system:

1. By creating a desire for the material blessings that the world offers.

2. By focusing our attention towards the honor and recognition of this world.
3. By making comfort and luxury as the basis for security.

There can be a "Delilah" in the life of every child of God- not necessarily a woman, but a weakness or a craving for the things and the pleasures of this world. The Bible says,

"Do not love the world, nor the things in the world. If anyone loves the world, the love of the father is not in him" (1 Jn. 2:15).

It was in the areas of the world and the flesh that satan won his original victory in the temptation of the first man and woman, and these are still his tactics today. Based on the foundation of the great victory won for us by Christ, you can defeat any attack from satan. Because of his defeat at the cross, the devil's only strength now is found in a Christian's ignorance (see Hos. 4:6). However, when a Christian knows the complete work of the cross and resurrection in his life, the devil is stripped of any weapon against him. Keep away from obvious areas of temptation. Do not set any vile thing before your eyes (see Ps. 101:3).

The Result of Samson's failure

Just as the Philistines gouged out Samson's eyes, and bound him with bronze chains, so does sin blind and bind people. It blinds them to their duty to God and to their fellow men, and prohibits them from doing anything about their blindness. When we sin we not only loose our power, but we also loose our peace. Pitifully, Samson did not know that his strength was gone. When Delilah had shaved the seven locks of his hair she said, *"The Philistines are upon you Samson!' [Samson then] awoke from his sleep and said, 'I will go out as at the other times and shake myself free.' But he did not know that the Lord had departed from him"* (Judg. 16:20).

We drift gradually into sin, hardly realizing that we've lost our strength until some crisis arises, and then we realize our weakness. Delilah cut off Samson's locks, and along life's pathway, many Delilahs cut off our power, peace, prayerfulness and position. Surely we must all take heed lest we fall. While in prison, while thinking of the mercies and blessings of the Lord, he must have surely repented of his sin and turned back to God.

One day the lords of the Philistines came together for a great feast. They came together to celebrate the capture and humiliation of their enemy, Samson. They began to eat and drink and be merry, giving their god, Dagon, the glory for their victory. As the feast moved to a climax they said, "Call for Samson, that he may amuse us." So they called for Samson from the prison and made him stand between two pillars. The house was full of men, women, and all the lords of the Philistines. Also, about 3,000 men and women were looking from the roof while Samson was amusing them. Samson asked a little boy who was holding his hand to help him feel the pillars on which the house rests, so that he could lean against them. Then Samson called out to God and said,

"O Lord God, please remember me and please strengthen me just this time, O God, that I may at once be avenged of the Philistines for my two eyes" (Judg. 16:28).

At the very least, he began to call upon God again, even if his motive was vengeance. God heard his prayer and supernaturally strengthened him one last time. He took hold of the two main pillars that held up the house and pulled on them with all his might. The house fell, killing not only Samson but also everyone in the house. The number he killed at his death were more than he killed in his lifetime (see Judg. 16:30).

Who - or what - is your Delilah? Loose relationships? Unforgiveness? Pride? You must locate it and deal with it in your life before it kills you. Samson was a Nazarite in outward appearance, but it is quite evident from the narrative that he knew little of the inward heart-separation to the Lord. He was not to touch or go near dead things. After he killed a lion, bees began to make honey in the dead body after awhile. Samson took the honey that was in the carcass of the dead lion and ate it, and gave some to his parents. He became ceremonially and spiritually unclean because he violated God's law not to touch dead things (see Judg. 14:8-9).

In the lives of believers there are things that God does not want us to touch or be involved in. These things can make us spiritually unclean. We should maintain our commitments and vows to the Lord and not fall into worldly living. However, early in his career, Samson began to compromise his anointing from God and to do things he was not supposed to do. Very slowly, he began to sow the seeds of his own destruction. When he ended up in a relationship with Delilah, which was forbidden by the law of God because she was a Philistine, it was not a surprise that she was able to trick him into revealing the secret of his power.

Don't ever let the devil steal the anointing from you like he did from Samson. Do not try to live in yesterday's anointing. Seek for a fresh anointing every day. We must do whatever it takes to keep in close touch with God. David says, "the nearness of God is my good" (Ps. 73:28).

In Samson the Nazarite we see a man towering in supernatural strength through his firm faith in, and confident reliance upon, the gift of God. On the other hand, we see in Samson an adventurous, foolhardy, passionate, and willful man, dishonoring and frittering away the God-given power by making it subservient to his own lusts. Moral weakness robs the strong man of both spiritual stature and physical prowess.

What a solemn warning we see in Samson's life, against playing with sin in any form! Just think of a judge of Israel in the lap of a Delilah, lulled by the devil, defeated, defiled, with his strength depleted and his sight gone! Yet Samson, with all his failings, is mentioned in Hebrews 11, which speaks of people of great faith. Only grace can do this for a man.

Despite all Samson's weaknesses, God used him. He is mentioned in the Bible *"Hall of Fame"* (see Heb. 11:32) as a hero of faith along with Gideon, Barak, and Jephthah, all from Judges.

Chapter 8

David Inhaled the Flame of Passion

David, the Old Testament songwriter, war hero, and head of state, was called a *"man after God's own heart."* (1 Sam.13:14; Acts 13:22). This was not the opinion of the Bible writers, who observed his life and character. The Lord Himself uttered that remarkable statement. God chose him for a definite purpose, to become Israel's greatest king and spiritual leader. The Lord called David from being a shepherd to the leadership of the people of Israel. The Almighty has no premium, or chromo, for laziness, but states plainly that faithfulness in lesser things shall pave the way to success in greater things.

Like Moses in the first half, David dominates the latter half of the Old Testament history. His exploits fill the books of 1 and 2 Samuel, and the songs he wrote can be found in the book of Psalms. All of the kings of Israel and Judah were measured against the standard he set during his forty-year reign. David was around fifty years old when he became king, and he had been Israel's king for about two decades. He was a gifted musician and a valiant warrior. Yet, he had a flaw in his character:

And David realized that the Lord had established him as king over Israel, and that He had exalted his kingdom for the sake of His people Israel. Meanwhile, David took more concubines and wives from Jerusalem, after he came from Hebron; and more sons and daughters were born to David (2 Sam. 5:12-13).

Polygamy violated the precepts God gave in Deuteronomy 17:17a.

David had a good heart and a broad mind. He had noble thoughts, and did noble deeds. He was a noble man and yet, his personality had a flaw. Thirsty as he was, he poured out on the ground the water, which three of his soldiers had brought him at the risk of their lives. He exclaimed that he could not drink it. He tried to cheer with his harp the man who hated him without a cause. He could not endure to listen to the narration of the ruin and death of his own bitter enemy. He had his worst foe and most powerful adversary in his power, and would not touch him. One of his captains called upon him to draw his sword and kill the man whom God had placed in his power, and he cried out, "God forbid!" When he at last became king, and the family of the man who had brought almost a lifetime of suffering and distress upon him was scattered, dethroned, destitute, or in the grave, he asked, "Is there any of the household of Saul left that I may show them kindness?" It is easy to understand why God said that David was a man after His own heart.

How Are The Mighty Fallen?

We see David, at one time, living close to God and serving him wholeheartedly. Then, we are greatly distressed and embarrassed to read of his great sin. Using his words, we too can say, "How are the mighty fallen?" During springtime when kings go out to battle, David stayed in Jerusalem and sent Joab and his servants with him and all Israel, and they destroyed the sons of Ammon and besieged Rabbah (2 Sam. 11:1). Fighting the battle for Israel was the responsibility given to David by God. But when the battle was raging, David was just relaxing at home, not keeping himself busy in the Lord's work. It was at this time that he indulged in the act of adultery. Truly, "an idle mind is the devil's workshop." Our greatest battles do not come when we are out working hard; they come when we have time on our hands. "Now when evening came, David arose from his bed and walked around on the roof of the king's house, and from the roof he saw a woman bathing; and the woman was very beautiful in appearance" (2 Sam. 11:2). One look at this beautiful woman and David's lust was inflamed.

When a sinful desire enters the mind, it will grow until the deed is executed, if it is not checked at once. As a rule, the mind eventually acts out what it dwells on. David is an example of this truth. First, he saw the beautiful woman bathing, and then he delighted in what he saw. We can call this "the second look." Always this second look is very dangerous. He allowed his mind to dwell on what he saw and the delight turned into desire, which we call lust. This desire brought about a decision to fulfill that lust and thus, he immediately sent messengers and inquired about the woman. One of them said that she was Bathsheba, the daughter of Eliam, the wife of Uriah the Hittite. David sent his messengers who brought her to him. David lay with her, and when she had purified herself, she returned to her house. He deliberately committed sin with Bathsheba, resulting in the death of her husband and of her first son, born through David. Because he did not nip temptation in the bud, he went on to put his thoughts into action, falling into sin.

Later, Bathsheba found out that she was pregnant, and sent word to David (2 Sam. 11:5). At that time, instead of facing his sin and confessing it before God and his counselors, David panicked and chose to develop a cover-up plan, trading his integrity for hypocrisy and deceit. David's plan was to bring Bathsheba's husband, Uriah, back from battle so that he would lie with his wife and assume that she had conceived his child. Then David sent word to Joab, saying, "Send me Uriah the Hittite." So Joab sent Uriah to David. When Uriah came to David he questioned him regarding the welfare of Joab, the people and the state of the war. David's questioning was not one of genuine concern but was mixed with hypocrisy. David told Uriah, "Go down to your house, and wash your feet" (2 Sam. 11:8). And Uriah went out of the king's presence and a present from the king was sent out after him. Sending a gift to Uriah was another ploy from David's deceitful hands. Nevertheless, David's efforts to get Uriah home to his wife didn't work. We read:

But Uriah slept at the door of the king's house with all the servants of his Lord, and did not go down to his house. Now when they told David saying, "Uriah did not go down to his house," David said to Uriah, "Have you not come from a journey? Why did you not go down to your house?" (2 Sam. 11:9-10)

Uriah's response to David must have pricked David's conscience with guilt, for he said to David, *"The ark and Israel and Judah are staying in temporary shelters, and my lord Joab and the servants of my Lord are camping in the open field. Shall I then go to my house to eat and to drink and to lie with my wife? By your life and the life of your soul, I will not do this thing"* (2 Sam. 11:11). Israelite soldiers had no sexual relations while they were preparing for battle (see 1 Sam. 21:5). Uriah refused to sleep with Bathsheba because he preferred duty before pleasure. He was one among the thirty-seven, a group of leading warriors under David (see 2 Sam. 23:39). David at last tried to get Uriah to go home to his wife. He wined and dined with him until he was drunk. But still, Uriah wouldn't go home, he went and laid on the bed of his lord's servant. Finally, David's cover up plan turned to cold-blooded murder. Uriah's single-minded devotion to duty spoiled David's plan. David rewarded Uriah with murder. The next morning, David sent a message with Uriah to Joab saying, *"Place Uriah in the front line of the fiercest battle and withdraw from him, so that he may be struck down and die"* (2 Sam. 11:15). David knew he would surely be killed. As a result of David's plan, Uriah, along with a number of other innocent soldiers, died. When the word of Uriah's death reached David, he sent a message to Joab saying, *"...do not let this thing displease you, for the sword devours one as well as another; make your battle against the city stronger and overthrow it, and so encourage him"* (2 Sam. 11:25). *"But the thing that David had done was evil in the sight of the Lord"* (2 Sam. 11: 27). Still David moved further along with his plan. When Bathsheba had finished grieving for her dead husband, David had her brought to his house and she became his wife; then she bore him a son. Although David had completely deceived the nation, he could not cover up his sin in God's eyes.

It always displeases God when we sin. David's sins of adultery, cold-blooded murder, and the subsequent cover up were an exceptional evil in God's sight. His sins were considered greater because he was a shepherd over God's people and the one who was responsible to administer justice and righteousness in Israel (see 2 Sam. 5:2; 8:15). In spite of all these things, it is surprising to see that David never seemed to show any initial sign of repentance, before Nathan confronts him. He tried to maintain integrity in the eyes of the people, and he could now enjoy Bathsheba as his wife... but he could not enjoy his fellowship with God.

In Second Samuel 12, God stirs David's heart toward repentance through the bold confrontation of Nathan. Wisely, Nathan approaches David indirectly, and cleverly captivates him with a heartrending story:

There were two men in one city, the one rich and the other poor. The rich man had a great many flocks and herds. But the poor man had nothing except one little ewe lamb, which he bought and nourished; and it grew up together with him and his children. It would eat of his bread and drink of his cup and lie in his bosom, and was like a daughter to him. Now a traveler came to the rich man, and he was unwilling to take from his own flock or his own herd, to prepare for the wayfarer who had come to him; rather he took the poor man's ewe lamb and prepared it for the man who had come to him (2 Sam. 12:1-4).

He offered the case to David, the highest judge in Israel. David's reaction was quick and powerful. His anger burned greatly against the man of whom Nathan was speaking about. He told Nathan, *"As the Lord lives, surely the man who has done this deserves to die"* (2 Sam. 12:5). Nathan tells David that he is the man in the story. The story was not really about a little lamb, but about David's cold-blooded murder of Uriah the Hittite. Nathan tells him,

> *Thus says the Lord God of Israel, "It is I who anointed you king over Israel and it is I who delivered you from the hand of Saul. I also gave you your master's house and your master's wives into your care, and I gave you the house of Israel and Judah; and if that had been too little, I would have added to you many more things like these!"* (2 Sam. 12:7-8)

He goes on to name David's crimes and their punishment, as told from the mouth of God. Broken over his sin, David confesses it to Nathan, saying, *"I have sinned against the Lord."* (2 Sam. 12:13). Nathan, the prophet of God, represents the convicting power of God's righteous Holy Spirit. In John 16:8 we read, *"And He, when He comes, will convict the world concerning sin, and righteousness, and judgment...."* The convicting work of the Holy Spirit is demonstrated clearly through Nathan, the prophet, as he confronts David about his sin against Bathsheba and Uriah. David's secret sin was uncovered and exposed to God's light-there was nowhere to hide. God sees everything.

However, Nathan told David that God has taken away his sin and he would not die. Nonetheless, God would take the life of his illegitimate son so that the Lord's enemies would have no reason to blaspheme God (see 2 Sam. 12:14). Nathan not only confronted David's sin, but he also named the painful consequences that the king would suffer.

The Consequences of David's Sin

David broke at least four of God's Ten Commandments in his sin with Bathsheba.

1.) He put the god of lust before the God of heaven.

2.) He coveted his neighbor's wife.

3.) He committed adultery.

4.) He indirectly murdered Uriah.

He was a great saint who committed a great sin. Sin hurts. What he did hurt his people. Sin hurts family, friends and above all, Jesus. David reaped a bitter harvest as a direct result of the things he did with Bathsheba. Even though he repented and found forgiveness, he still had to face those consequences. Deep down we think that if we confess our sin fast enough we will be saved from all of the suffering it brings. God's dealing with David reminds us that this is not the case. God is not being unfair when he allows the consequences of our sins to bring our lives to a screeching halt. By doing so the Lord reaffirms His love for us, a love so great that He will do whatever it takes to deliver us from the grip of a sinful involvement.

David faced the consequence of his sin soon after it was predicted. The Lord struck the son Bathsheba bore to David with a sickness. On the seventh day of the boy's sickness, the child died (see 2 Sam. 12:15-18). The word of the Lord, spoken through the prophet Nathan when he confronted David of his adultery with Bathsheba, came true:

Now therefore, the sword shall never depart from your house, because you have despised me and have taken the wife of Uriah the Hittite to be your wife... I will raise up evil against you from your own household; I will even take your wives before your eyes, and give them to your companion, and he shall lie with your wives in broad daylight. Indeed you did it secretly, but I will do this thing before all Israel, and under the sun (2 Sam. 12:10-12).

Sin deceives. David gave in to sin, he began to walk down sin's slippery slope of destruction that began with giving in to lust, plots, lies, schemes, intrigue, cover-ups, and finally murder! Although God forgave David and he genuinely repented, his sins cost him very dearly.

You may ask the question, "Are you telling me I don't have to sin?" My reply is, "Where did you ever get the idea that you have to sin?" We read in First John 2:1, "*My dear children, I write this to you so that you will not sin. But if anybody does sin, we have one who speaks to the Father in our defense- Jesus Christ, the Righteous One."* God does not refer to us in scripture as sinners but as saints and as a royal priesthood. But still we may sin only when we choose to sin.

Has sin disappeared or lost its power because we are dead to sin and alive to God? No, it is still strong and still appealing. But when sin makes its appeal, we have the power to say no to it because our relationship with sin ended when the Lord rescued us from the dominion of darkness and brought us into the Kingdom of Light (see Col. 1:12-13). Paul explains how this is possible in Romans 8:1-2: *"Therefore, there is now no condemnation for those who are in Christ Jesus, because through Christ Jesus the law of the Spirit of life set me free from the law of sin and death."* It is true that the law of sin and death is still in operation in this world, because it is a law. But the greater law of the Spirit of life has overcome it. I would like to illustrate this truth by comparing it to flying in an airplane.

Ever since I was born, I have been bound to this earth by a law that I have never been able to break - the law of gravity. But we all know that there is another law, which is a higher law - the law of aero-dynamics. If only I am willing to commit myself in total trust to this higher law of aero-dynamics, then I will be set free from the law of gravity. This also changes my condition. Now, by faith I step into the plane and I just sit and rest on my seat in faith and as those powerful engines roar into life, I discover that the new law of aerodynamics sets me free from the law of gravity. As long as I maintain, by faith, that position of total dependence, I do not have to try to be free from the law of gravity. I am kept free by the operation of a new and a higher law. If I feel stuffy and uncomfortable as the plane crosses the Atlantic or Pacific Ocean, and I suddenly decide to step out through the emergency window, what happens then? The moment I discard my position in this new law, I discover that the old, down-dragging law is still in full operation, and I am caught again by this law of gravity and would plunge into the ocean. I must maintain my attitude of dependence if I am to remain airborne! I would like to compare the airplane with Jesus.

After accepting Jesus as your Lord and Saviour, you have positioned yourself in Christ. Now you are inside the plane and you come under the law of aerodynamics (the law of spirit of life). Paul says, "Sin shall have no dominion over you." Likewise the law of gravity should not have dominion over you. It is true that the law of gravity (the law of sin and death) is still operative, still powerful, and still making its appeal. But you don't need to submit to it. The law of the spirit of life is a greater law. As long as you live by the Spirit, you will not carry out the desires of the flesh (see Gal. 5:16). Someone has said, "TB affects the lungs; TV affects the heart." When temptation knocks, send Jesus to the door.

She Thought, "It's just a bite"
But oh! What cosmic bait
Eve bit more than what she could chew
Indigestion dogs you and me.

He thought, "It's just a stare"
But oh! His life became a nightmare
David stayed and didn't go to fight
To Bathsheba, lost his moral might.

He thought, "I will keep the plunder"
But oh! His life was torn asunder
Achan thought none knew what he hid
Paid a heavy price for what he did

He thought, "It's just a one-night stay"
But oh! What a cost he did pay
Samson was Delilah's poor prey
Died bound and blind, coz of sinful stray.

Friend, "Don't give Devil a foothold"
He'll usher in miseries untold
Stand firm; unsheathe the Spirit's sword
Stay strong in the armour of God. (PRABHU SINGH)

David's Honest Confession

David responded to Nathan's confrontation with a wholehearted confession: *"I have sinned against the Lord."* (2 Sam. 12:13). David was a great king partly because he did not act with the normal pride of a king. He was humble. When confronted with the truth, he repented. David acknowledged his sin. He accepted the truth and the seriousness of what he had done and why it had happened, which is so important for recovery. The memory of it was part of what would protect him from another such failure. He said, *"For I know my transgressions, and my sin is ever before me"* (Ps. 51:3). He cried out for mercy, pleading with God to purify his heart. *"Purify me with hyssop, and I shall be clean; Wash me and I shall be whiter than snow"* (Ps. 51:7). His words show us the true nature of confession when he cried out, *"Against Thee, Thee only, have I sinned, and done this evil in Thy sight, so that Thou mightest be justified when Thou speakest, and clear when Thou judgest"* (Ps. 51:4). David faced the consequences realistically. He told his officials, *"While the child was still alive, I fasted and wept; for I said, 'Who knows, the Lord may be gracious to me, that the child may live.' But now he has died; why should I fast? Can I bring him back again? I shall go to him, but he will not return to me."* David accepted this painful consequence, refusing to blame God or become bitter (2 Sam. 12:22-23).

David's response shows that he believed in the hope of heaven. He knew his son was gone, but he also knew that one day he would see him again. Even in the midst of his suffering, David relied on God's truth. Then David comforted his wife Bathsheba and lay with her and she gave birth to a son, and he named him Solomon (see 2 Sam. 12:24). David felt the pangs of sin deeply and was earnest in his repentance. Sincc God looks at the intentions of the heart, David could be called *"a man after His own heart"* (1 Sam. 13:14). God is concerned more with who we are than with what we do.

First and Second Samuel does not paint him as a flawless character, nor as a perfect model of strength and courage. David had striking weaknesses. In his love for God, he held nothing back. David knew that God loved him even though his sin had caused death and destruction for many.

Psalm 103:12 states, *"As far as the east is from the west, so far has He removed our transgressions from us."* God is bigger than our sins, and even though there are times when we will have to experience pain and suffering for our choices in life, we can count on the fact that God holds nothing against us if we ask for His forgiveness. Nevertheless, David was Israel's greatest king. Even at his lowest points, his great strength of character showed. He never sought to exert vengeance on enemies. He took full responsibility for his mistakes. Perhaps he always remembered that he had started out as a mere shepherd. He held power only by the grace of God and he believed that God had every right to take power away.

In conclusion, there is only one thing to say: Fear God and obey his commandments, because this is all that man was created for. God is going to judge everything we do, whether good or bad, including things done in secret. We are to resist the temptation that comes to us from the world by allowing God to transform us by the renewing of our minds, that we may prove His perfect will for us (see Rom. 12:1-2). But when it comes from the devil, Scripture says, *"Submit yourselves, therefore, to God. Resist the devil, and he will flee from you."* For the believer, there is this promise:

"Blessed is the man that endures temptation; for when he has been approved, he will receive the crown of life which the Lord has promised to those who love Him" (Jas. 1:12).

Above all, be sure that your personal relationship with Jesus Christ is alive and growing. If, thus far, you have not committed your life to Jesus Christ, do it right now, and what He accomplished on the cross when He paid for your sin will be credited to your account. Then submit yourself to God, resist the devil, and you will overcome temptation. May the Lord help you to live a victorious Christian life!

Chapter 9
Boundaries for Self Control

The Oxford Dictionary defines "boundaries" as "lines marking limits of land." Regarding this study, it means the lines marking the limits established by God in the lives of humans. Certainly the Bible contains rules, principles, and stories that explain what it is like to exist on this earth.

In the spiritual world, boundaries are just as real, but often harder to see. The boundaries define our souls, and they help us to guard it and maintain it (see Prov. 4:23). We have to deal with what is in our souls, and boundaries help us to define what that is.

Why Do We Need Boundaries?

God respects our boundaries in many ways. First, He allows us to do what we feel like doing and then, He allows us to experience the painful consequences of our behavior, so that we will change. God is not willing for any one of us to perish, and He takes no pleasure in our destruction (see 2 Pet.3:9; Ezek. 18:23), but He always wants us to change for our own good and ultimately, for His glory. It hurts Him deeply when we don't. However, at the same time, He does not rescue us. He wants us to work it out for our own good. He will plead with us to come back to Him. He does this because of His mercy toward us. Hence, we should endeavour not to go beyond the boundaries He has set. Secondly, He respects our "no". He tries neither to control nor nag us. He allows us to say "no" and go our ways. Recall the stories of Jonah, the prodigal son, the rich young ruler, and the story of Joshua and his people. In all these examples, God gives a choice and allows the people involved to decide for themselves. When people say no, He allows it and still loves them. He is a giver. One of the things God always gives is a choice, but like a real giver, He also allows the consequences of those choices to unfold. He respects boundaries.

Even though the people of Israel were called as God's own people, still God made a boundary in terms of approaching Him. But for Moses, there were no limits or boundaries to go to God. It gives a clear understanding that all people are not worthy of reaching the standard, which God has set for us. You should not go up the mountain or touch the foot of it. God is Holy and those who approach him should be holy. The people of Israel did not go to touch the mountain. Because of man's unholiness, a rift has occurred between he and God (see Ex. 19:12).

Many clinical psychological symptoms such as depression, anxiety disorders, eating disorders, addictions, impulsive disorders, guilt problems, shame issues, panic disorders, and marital and relational struggles find their root in conflicts with established boundaries. Boundaries help us differentiate where individuals begin and end in relationships. These boundaries are defined by the way we speak, use our time, money, privileges, and so on. We shall deal with two such boundaries, namely, sexuality, and alcohol and substance abuse.

Sexuality

First of all we must understand what the Bible talks about sex. It is holy in the sight of God. It is created and ordained by God (see Gen. 2:24). The Bible says,

"May your fountain be blessed, and may you rejoice in the wife of your youth. A loving doe, a graceful deer-may her breasts satisfy you always, may you ever be captivated by her love" (Prov. 5:18-19).

Paul said to abstain from sexual immorality (see Acts 15:20).

God gave us sexual desire both to reproduce ourselves and to enjoy our spouses. People who are addicted to pornography have diverted this good desire into a perverted form of sexuality given by the world. The problem with most of internal boundary conflicts is that sexual boundaries become a tyrant, demanding and insatiable. No matter how many orgasms are reached, the desire only deepens, and the inability to say no to one's lusts drives one deeper into despair and hopelessness. Many people try to make decisions about their sexuality in times of intense emotional and physical attraction. At that point of time, it is very difficult to be object and to stay within the boundaries.

Alcohol And Substance Abuse

Alcohol and drug abuses have devastated several lives. Divorce, job loss, financial havoc, medical problems, and death are the fruits of the inability to set limits in these areas. We become our own worst enemies. You have to switch your focus from setting limits on other people to setting limits on yourself. When you meet someone who finds fault with everything, you can set limits on your exposure to this person's constant criticism. But what if this critical person is in your own head? What if you are the person with the problem? What if you have met the enemy, and he is you?

Some people withdraw from relationships when they most need them. Since the fall of man, our instincts have been to withdraw from relationship when we're in trouble, when we most need other people. (Remember how Adam and Eve hid from God after they ate the forbidden fruit?) Due to our lack of security, our loss of grace, our shame, and our pride, we turn inward, rather than outward, when we're in trouble. The Bible says,

"Woe to one who is alone and falls and does not have another to help" (see Eccl. 4:10).

How Do Boundaries Help Us?

Boundaries help us to define what is not on our property and what we are not responsible for. Only if you are able to distinguish your property can you properly take care of it. They help you to "guard your heart with all diligence." You need boundaries to help you keep the good in and bad out. They guard your treasures so that people will not steal them (see Matt. 7:6). They keep the pearls inside and the pigs outside.

For example, if you find that you have some pain or sin within, you need to open up and communicate it to God and others, so that you can be healed. God always expects this. Confessing pain and sin helps to "get it out" so that it does not continue to poison you on the inside (see 1 Jn. 1:9; Jas. 5:16; Mk. 7: 21-23). God expects His boundaries to be respected. Boundaries help you to be the best you can be in God's image and they help you see God as He really is. They enable you to live your life according to God's will, fulfilling your responsibilities and requirements.

Internal Boundary Conflicts

Whether your boundary issue is food, substances, sex, time, projects, the tongue, or money, you can't solve it in a vacuum. The more you isolate yourself, the harder your struggle becomes. Just like the untreated cancer that can become life threatening in a short time, maintaining personal boundaries will be more difficult with increased isolation. You should look at your responsibility to control your own body instead of looking at the control and manipulation of others (see 1 Thess. 4:4). Instead of examining outer boundary conflicts with other people, you should be looking at your own internal boundary conflicts. Keep yourself open to the comments, suggestions, and feedback from others.

You should not depend on your willpower to solve your boundary problems. The problem with the willpower approach is that it makes an idol out of the will, something God never intended. Just as our hearts and minds are distorted by the fall, so is our power to make right decisions. Will is only strengthened by relationships- you can't make commitments alone. God told Moses to encourage and strengthen Joshua (see Deut 3:28); he didn't tell Moses to tell Joshua to "just say no." If you depend on willpower alone, you may fail because you are denying the power of the relationship promised in the cross. If all you need is your will to overcome evil, you certainly don't need a Savior (see 1 Cor. 1:17). The truth is, willpower alone is useless in maintaining personal boundaries.

It is not easy to become mature in self-boundaries. Many obstacles hinder our progress. However, God desires our maturity and self-control even more than we do. He's on our team as an Exhorter, Encourager, and Implorer (see 1 Thess: 2:11-12). Think about the destructive fruit you may be exhibiting by not being able to say no to yourself. You may be experiencing depression, anxiety, panic, phobias, rage, relationship struggles, isolation, work problems, or psychosomatic problems. Identifying the causes of your self-boundary problems will help you understand your own contribution to the problem.

Chapter 10

How To Overcome Online Temptation

The greatest temptation today for the young and the old alike is to browse through pornographic images online or share intimate fantasies in chat rooms. In the beginning it may seem like harmless entertainment, but eventually it can lead to addictive and compulsive behaviors that would damage relationships in the real world.

Online Fantasies Affect Healthy Behavior

Online fantasies have lured away many from their spouses and have already destroyed many marriages. All that I am sharing in this article is from what I have discovered during my counseling sessions of both young and the middle-aged people. Many have confessed that online sex has left in them mental and emotional scars that have changed their understanding of sexuality and have become a hindrance in maintaining a normal marital relationship. It has greatly affected the healthy behavior of many young people. Pornography has pulled many out of a normal lifestyle into a world of addiction and violence. The main purpose of this article is to help you refocus your energies spent on disrupted and damaged relationships

At the end of the day can online sex really satisfy you? The very fact that you feel guilty when you log off your computer, after viewing pornography, shows you that God is not pleased. As you continue your involvement in online sex, you may start to realize that there is a struggle in relating to your spouse. Your love may grow cold. You may feel like pulling away from people and activities in real life. These are the symptoms of abnormality that arise from online sex. As Internet pioneer Clifford Stoll says, "Life in the real world is far more interesting, far more important, and far richer than anything you'll ever find on a computer screen." Business executives, professionals, pastors, and leaders may be especially vulnerable to online sexual problems because of the demands and loneliness often associated with professionalism and ministry.

Are you looking for a solution to your problems in chat rooms or on pornographic web sites? Or are you are looking for love, nurture, relationship, excitement, and fulfillment in sex through these websites? You will never get anywhere near to the solution, but will instead become lost in an endless cycle of fantasy, sexual indulgence, guilt, and despair.

Pornography causes massive damage in your life and in relationships with others. King Solomon once said, "Can a man scoop fire into his lap without his clothes being burned?" (Proverbs 6:27) Similarly, can you repeatedly bring sexually arousing images into your head without consequences? You may not be physically burned by sexual images, but psychologists say that those images can actually be burned into your mind. Emotional arousal causes the release of a hormone called epinephrine in your brain that chemically records the pictures into your permanent memory. This effect is further heightened by the combination of pictures and masturbation. Sometimes, pornography can even lead you to do things you never imagined. The fantasy world of pornography can only put you into a lonely roller coaster of excitement and emptiness. God created us with a natural desire for love and intimacy that can only be filled in a relationship with Him and, to some degree, through a special relationship with our respective spouses.

Sex on the Internet Can Never be Fulfilling

Sex on the Internet can never be as fulfilling as sex with your spouse in the "real world." Sex on the Internet or any sexual indulgence portrayed through any media is given by the devil. But, God has designed and given to us the sexual fulfillment within the marriage relationship. Disappointment with a spouse is one of the most convenient and popular excuses used by those messing around in sexual sin. An unsatisfying, cold, sexual relationship with a spouse is not an excuse to turn to pornography. Such an excuse is just a rationalization that some use to attempt to avoid their personal responsibilities within the marriage covenant. It is the sin in your heart and the wrong choices that you make that drive you to sexual compromise.

Sexual fulfillment is a part of the intimate relationship of marriage for which God has created us as man and woman. God created us as whole persons to experience sex in relationships, which involve the whole person. You should never risk the potential pain and disappointment that would possibly forever affect the real relationship. You should not dare to dive into a fantasy world that is merely a shadow of what God created us to experience.

Can Intimacy be Found Online?

A major excuse that people give for going into sex sites online is to find intimacy. But can intimacy be found online? It depends on your definition of intimacy. Some people simply define intimacy as sex. By that definition, there's plenty of intimacy online filled with sexual images and stories as well as scores of high-tech virtual sex services. This kind of content can easily lead to sexual stimulation, but it cannot develop real intimacy.

The dictionary defines intimacy as very close association, a warm familiarity with, et cetera. A broad range of online personalities may draw closer enough to their viewers only to get into their wallets but would not share an intimate meaningful love relationship, as a spouse would do. Dr. James Dobson says, "Men tend to give intimacy in order to get sex and women tend to give sex in order to get intimacy."

Some people take advantage of the online interaction because it hides all of their weaknesses while exaggerating their strengths. A true intimacy requires a tremendous amount of face-to-face interaction in the real world, where we are able to put everything on the table. Only then we can process non-verbal communication, interpret emotions, and truly evaluate our life styles.

True intimacy can exist only when we are prepared to show the other person unconditional love. Eventually we all need someone who can still love us when we are not at our best-when we are sick, unattractive, or have made mistakes.

Discover God's Intended Relationship

Working on the marriage may require a lot of painful examination and intensive emotional effort. But turning to pornography is a dangerous and a sinful way out. The spouses should strive to develop self-surrendering, tender, loving, sacrificial need, based upon open and honest communication. Hence, the most important factor in overcoming sexual temptation and finding fulfillment with your spouse is discovering the relationship that God has intended for the two of you to have. You must overcome your desire to control your spouse. You must be willing to be painfully honest in trying to learn and identify your spouse's needs, thereby find ways to lovingly, continually, and purposely meet those needs. Developing such a mutual understanding in enhancing the joy of an intimate relationship with your spouse helps keep you away from desiring another man or woman.

The Roadmap to Recovery

A. Realize that You are in the Danger Zone.

When sexual temptation has a hold on you and sexual sin has become a sad reality in your life, healing is necessary and will only take place through a realization that you are in the danger zone. You must first of all whole-heartedly confess it before the Lord.

B. Share Your Struggle With Someone Who Can Help You.

Your resolve to come out of it in your own strength will not work. It doesn't matter what kinds of sexual activities you have been involved in. However perverse, offensive, or sinful, the Lord loves you deeply and He longs to be gracious to you and waits to have compassion on you (Isa.30: 18). God demonstrated His unconditional love and forgiveness for you by sending His own Son, Jesus Christ, to take the punishment for all of your lustful thoughts and actions. Believing in the healing power of Christ's love is the most effective way to overcome the sense of shame that you have had in you.

Sexual problems are often intensified when they are kept secret. Sharing your struggles with others provides an opportunity for accountability as well as reflection on underlying problems. Psalm 32:3 says,

"When I kept silence, my bones grew old through my groaning all the day long."

Find a mature friend or a fellow believer and talk about your sin and your struggle to that person. Moving towards renewal is not a simple process. Recovery requires a combination of accountability, counseling, and spiritual reflection.

If you are a married person, you must realize that God brought you both together for an intimate relationship with each other. To live in a relationship filled with unconfessed sin, secret struggles, and hidden failures is anything but intimate. Honest confession may lead to a period of profound pain and disappointment, but without total transparency and full disclosure, the marriage cannot be authentic and will never become the type of relationship that God desires for us. In fact, your spouse can be one of your most valuable means of accountability and may provide you with strong solutions, significant strength and motivation to save you from falling into these temptations.

C. Get Out of Your Lonliness

Looking for healthy relationships is the key. You especially need relationships that bring accountability. You will also need spiritual support. While you try to develop your relationship with God, it will be very helpful if you spend time with others who are pursuing the same goal in their lives. There are some people who make strong decisions not to drink or smoke. But they keep cigarettes or bottles of alcohol in their storeroom. Guess what. They will never quit for long because they have easy access to cigarettes or drinks when the cravings get strong. If you ever get serious about quitting smoking or drinking, you will have to get rid of your cigarettes and bottles of alcohol.

D. Eliminate Easy Access

One way you can reduce the temptation is to cut back on the number of "gateway images" you expose yourself to, especially TV, movies, sensual magazines, and heavy metal and rock music. If you know that a particular sitcom causes your mind to wander to sexual fantasies, it's time to cut it off. *"Flee the evil desires of youth, and pursue righteousness, faith, love and peace, along with those who call on the Lord out of a pure heart"* (2 Timothy 2:22).

If sexual sin has been your struggle, you need to get rid of your stash and eliminate easy access. This is the challenge of "living in the world" but not "being of the world." We must face the reality that we are "strangers in a strange land." In this regard, I would like to draw your attention to the seals that live in the sea. Although they are known to be expert swimmers, it is not inherent in their nature. The Encyclopedia Britannica, 1963 edition, declares, "Seals are taught to swim by their parents." Born on the rocks but destined to live in the sea, they must lcarn how to live in a world so different from the one into which they were born. Likewise, although we are born into the natural world, we are destined to live in the spiritual world. Our time on the land is short; our full lives should be lived in the sea of God's kingdom. Though we are not born with an inherent ability to relate to or respond in that world, we have to be taught.

Everything in God's world is foreign to us. Even though we may possess a strong desire for holiness, we lack any innate ability to produce that holiness. So, my friend, you may remain on the rock until someone teaches you how to swim. That is the work of the Holy Spirit of God. He will gently lead you from your natural world to His supernatural world. When submarines descend deep into the ocean, they encounter dramatic changes in the pressures surrounding them. A submarine would fold like tin foil from the weight of the water were it not for internal pressurization. The internal pressure must be equal to that on the outside; otherwise, the external pressure will collapse the walls.

E. Your Mind With Godly Stuff

Even after putting an end to viewing sexual images online, some people find it difficult to get those old images out of their head as they try to restore relationship with their spouses. Although viewing pornography is like digging trenches in the mind and filling it with junk, God can certainly remove the junk and bring restoration. At the same time, you need to fill the trenches with positive and Godly stuff. A heart committed to Christ and a mind soaking in the things of Christ provides powerful, life-changing energy. The Bible is a great place to start. Christian music, devotional material, Christian magazines, regular attendance at worship services, joining a small group, and reading Christian books are some of the means by which you can positively feed your mind.

We need to pursue righteousness. This includes working actively to replace sexual images in your mind with more wholesome, holy thoughts.

"Finally, brothers, whatever is true, whatever is noble, whatever is right, whatever is pure, whatever is lovely, whatever is admirable-if anything is excellent or praiseworthy-think about such things" (Philippians 4:8).